Research Centre for the History of Religious and Cultural Diversity
(Meiji University, Tokyo)

Memory and Narrative Series 9

The Life Story of Mrs Nilima Devi, MBE: An Indian Classical Dancer in Leicester

Edited and written by Kiyotaka Sato

Foreword by Mr Christopher Maughan, former Principal Lecturer and Research Fellow, De Montfort University

This memory and narrative series is published by Kiyotaka Sato, Professor of European History, School of Arts and Letters, Meiji University, Tokyo. The purpose of the project is to enable the UK's many and various ethnic minority communities and indigenous groups to record and preserve their memories, life experiences and traditions, and to ensure access to this rich inheritance for present and future generations. The project is established with financial support from the Meiji University as well as the Ministry of Education, Culture, Sports, Science and Technology (Japan) and other organisations.

First published by RCHRCD, July 2016

Copyright © 2016 Kiyotaka Sato

Research Centre for the History of Religious and Cultural Diversity (RCHRCD)
Meiji University, Tokyo
1-1 Kandasurugadai, Chiyoda-ku,
Tokyo, 101-8301, Japan
Email: satokiyo@meiji.ac.jp

All rights reserved. No part of this publication may be reproduced, stored in a retrieval system, or transmitted in any form, or by any means, electronic, mechanical, photo-copying, recording or otherwise, without the prior permission in writing of the author. Enquiries concerning reproduction outside these terms and in other countries should be sent to the editor at the address above.

Outside front cover:
  Mrs Nilima Devi
  (Reproduced with the permission of Mrs Nilima Devi)
Inside front cover:
  Mrs Nilima Devi
  (Reproduced with the permission of Mrs Nilima Devi)
Outside back cover:
  Mrs Nilima Devi and her family
  (Reproduced with the permission of Mrs Nilima Devi)

ISSN 2185-6079

Published Asia Printing Office Corporation
Address: 1154 Miwa araya, Nagano-shi, Nagano, 380-0804, Japan

Acknowledgements

I wish to thank the following people and organisations who assisted me with my work:

Mrs Delia Baker
Mrs Nilima Devi's family
Mr Richard Bettsworth (former editor, Leicester Mercury)
Mr Kevin Booth (Editor, Leicester Mercury)
Emeritus Professor Richard Bonney, University of Leicester
Mrs Margaret Bonney (former Chief Archivist, Record Office for Leicestershire, Leicester & Rutland)
Mrs Cynthia Brown (former Project Manager of the East Midlands Oral History Archive [EMOHA], University of Leicester)
Mr Nick Carter (former Editor, Leicester Mercury)
Mr Steve England (former Archivist, Leicester Mercury)
Associate Professor Jun Fukushi, Okayama University
Mrs Yoshimi Gregory (Chair, Leicestershire Japan Society)
Associate Professor Jenny Holt, Meiji University
Mr Asaf Hussain (Chairperson of the Society for Intercultural Understanding)
Mrs Freda Hussain (former Principal of Moat Community College)
Mr Colin Hyde (Researcher and outreach officer of the East Midlands Oral History Archive [EMOHA], University of Leicester)
Mr Shuichi Kurosaki (part-time lecturer, Meiji University)
Mr Christopher Maughan, former Principal Lecturer and Research Fellow, De Montfort University
Emeritus Professor Werner Menski, School of Oriental and African Studies (SOAS), University of London
Emeritus Professor Eleanor Nesbitt, University of Warwick
Mrs Sonia Spencer
Dr Pippa Virdee, Senior Lecturer, De Montfort University

The Centre for Indian Classical Dance (CICD)
Leicester Central Library
Leicester City Council
Leicester Mercury
University of Leicester
De Montfort University
Record Office for Leicestershire, Leicester & Rutland

Above all I wish to thank Mrs Nilima Devi whom I interviewed and, who gave me much other information about her life story.

Foreword

The series of nine biographical studies that Professor Kiyotaka Sato has written on the lives of selected people living in Leicester provides an important and fascinating insight into how individuals can help to shape the community in which they live, work and play. The fact that his chosen subjects are all residents of Leicester is of particular interest as Leicester is one of the UK's most diverse and multicultural cities. The 2011 UK Census suggests that it may be the first city in which those indicating that they are White British form less than 50% of the population.

Providing another backdrop to Professor Sato's series are the wider issues of immigration and cultural identity which are currently receiving much attention in the UK, where the Conservative government has chosen to offer the country a referendum on its continuing membership of the European Union. The referendum has been underwhelming as the campaigns of the two main groups, Brexit (Leave It) and Remain (Better Together), have focused largely on economic issues such as employment and overseas trade. Despite the anxiety in some quarters about lack of control of immigration, little attention has been given to one of the most significant features of Europe, its social and cultural history.

This is in contrast to one of the key features of the 'Memory and Narrative Series' which is to draw attention to the close relationship between an individual's moral and cultural compass and the standing they have in the immediate and wider community context in which their lives and work are embedded. Ramanbhai Barber captures this well in his contribution to Booklet No 8 when he discusses the concept of Seva or 'selfless service'. Nilima Devi's life is a good example of this concept in action.

It has been my pleasure to have known and worked with Nilima Devi for over 20 years and to have been a trustee of the Centre for Indian Classical Dance (CICD) for more than 10 of them. This has given me many opportunities to witness her own 'selfless service' to dance and to Kathak and other classical Indian dance forms in particular. Her service has been recognised formally by her selection as one of the Midlands Champions of Culture in 2012 and subsequently through the award of the MBE for her services to dance in 2013. These are however the tip of the iceberg in terms of the influence she has had upon those with whom she has worked, entertained, and supported since she left India in 1979.

Her achievements and, through her, the achievements of CICD are impressive:

As a cultural ambassador of Indian/South Asian dance in the East Midlands she has reached more than 100,000 people in her role as an artist and teacher through schools, colleges, communities, adult and higher education, festivals, performing at mainstream venues, and by regular teaching at CICD as well as through outreach programmes.

Her 'career', or perhaps vocation is a more apt word, includes visits to over 600 schools and colleges, 1,040 weekly training classes at her studio in Churchill Street, Leicester, from where she has taught over 2,500 students of various ages, many of whom have been submitted for the Diploma in Dance examination. In addition to this hectic schedule she has also managed to produce 475 dance shows, including 400 community showcases and 75 professional touring shows.

Celebrated highlights include a dance drama based on Hans Christian Andersen's fairy tale *The Ugly Duckling*, showcases such as *Seasons of India, American Dream, Aladdin, Stars and Stripes, Rainbow, Kathak Katha, Melory, The Jungle Book*, and a Kathak rendition of *Beethoven's Piano Concerto No 1*. Other highlights of artistic productivity and cross-cultural collaboration have been a project entitled *Flaming Feet*, in which Nilima combined Irish dance and music, with Indian dance and music, as well as a wide range of other choreographic work which featured other Indian and Asian dancers brought to Leicester from around the world.

And to further underline the extent of her enthusiasm, Nilima has also overseen the production and distribution of several books, e.g. *Karman*, and a DVD, *Sinjini*, which provide additional insights into the richness of the culture that she has presented so well on stages around the world.

But who is the person who has delivered so much?

This book reveals how in 1980 the young NiIima Devi (she was born in 1953) came to Leicester with her husband Werner and young son, from her home in Baroda, Gujarat, where she had begun her lifelong devotion to Kathak.

The qualities that she possessed then and which set her out on her unique journey are still visible today and the ones that have struck me particularly are:

- Her skill in recognising others' strengths and talent and her ability to develop them as artists and people
- Her encouragement of more advanced performers, some of whom now work at national and international levels
- Her deep personal knowledge and understanding of Indian classical dance and music traditions – and her ability to enthuse others to develop their own knowledge and skill
- Her active participation within many community based programmes which have contributed significantly to community cohesion
- Her status and quality as one of this country's most creative and innovative dancers and choreographers of Asian classical dance, Asian community and folk dance and other contemporary and popular forms such as Bollywood.

She has drawn on these qualities and her solid academic and practical foundations to develop and deliver a South Asian dance (and arts) experience that few others would be able to achieve to the same high level.

Nilima's focus and commitment are singular features of her personality which in turn are drawn from her devotion to her family, her culture, her religion and her community. It is her capacity to retain her personal and cultural identity whilst working in the highly competitive environment of the cultural scene in the UK that is perhaps one of her greatest legacies.

At a time when a materialistic celebrity culture is a dominant feature of the cultural offer in the UK and Europe, Nilima serves as a reminder that other cultural reference points can provide an alternative perspective on what is important and may serve as a source of values to follow. She reminds us that culture can be inclusive as well as exclusive, that culture provides a foundation for how we interact with others from different cultural traditions, and encourages respect for all culture as a source of knowledge, a way of seeing and a way of being: a way of life.

This book is a testament to a life that has been lived to the full and in which she still continues to push the boundaries. Through her dedication to Kathak and related dance forms, and her work as performer and teacher, Nilima has developed in others a deep interest in the culture that nurtured the form, but within a contemporary context. This quality she has passed on to many others, as noted by Aakash Odedra, one of her many students and now a professional dancer who performs around the world.

The decision that she made in 1976 to forgo the siren call of the banking industry means that its loss has been to the benefit of the individuals, the wider communities of Leicester and the East Midlands where she has given over 30 years of service. It is hoped that her story will, as she writes herself *'inspire others to become involved in work that they believe to be useful and conducive to making this world a better place'*. 'Selfless service' has had few better exponents.

Christopher Maughan
West Kilbride, Scotland
May 2016

CONTENTS

Acknowledgements 5

Foreword 6

I. Introduction 11
II. The Life Story of Mrs Nilima Devi, MBE 17
    1 My birthplace and my family background 18
    2 Learning Indian classical dance and my work career ... 20
    3 My marriage 22
    4 Moving to Germany, and my life in Germany 25
    5 Moving to England and to Leicester 26
    6 My children's education and their marriage 28
    7 Teaching Indian classical dance in Leicester 32
    8 Nilima Devi's MBE 36
    9 Systematic education in Indian classical dance and musical instruments 37
    10 Hindu festivals and the history of Indian classical dance ... 38
    11 Differences of Indian classical dance between north India and south India 40
    12 Differences between Indian classical dance and Bollywood dance ... 40
    13 Leicester as a multi-ethnic city 43
    14 Asian dance in Leicester in the twenty-first century ... 44
III. Addendum to the book on Nilimaji 51
    My perspectives on why we are, and remain, in Leicester: Werner Menski 52
IV. Appendices 59
    Appendix 1: Nilima Devi in India and wedding 60
    Appendix 2: Coming to Germany, settling in England, and family

visits	69
Appendix 3: Teaching Indian classical dance in Leiceseter	72
Appendix 4: Performance and dance activities of Nilima Devi	91
Appendix 5: Nilima Devi's MBE	125
Appendix 6: Dance posters and leaflets	129
Appendix 7: Memories by Nilima Devi's students (Aakash Odedra; Gita Lakhlani)	154
Appendix 8: Reflections on the *Parampara* and *Karman* projects (Colin Hyde; Cynthia Brown)	162
Appendix 9: The history of the Indian classical dance in Leicester (Extracts from the *Leicester Mercury*)	165
Appendix 10: Ethnicity and Religion in the UK and Leicester	181
Appendix 11: Maps of the Gujarat state of India, Germany and Leicester in the UK	192
Appendix 12: Select bibliography and websites	195
Appendix 13: Message from Mrs Nilima Devi, MBE	201

I
Introduction

I   Introduction

Introduction

The subject of this volume, the ninth in the Memory and Narrative Series, is the Indian dancer and teacher Nilima Devi. She was born in 1953 in Vadodara (formerly Baroda) in Gujarat State, India. After marrying her German husband in 1979, Nilima left India for the German city of Bochum, where she stayed for around eighteen months. Then, in September 1980, she migrated to England and settled permanently in Leicester. There, in the following year, she founded the Centre for Indian Classical Dance (CICD), and in 1985 she became a classical dance animateur, a role created by a partnership of local agencies, and taught in schools and neighbourhood centres. Through her work at CICD, and in her role both as a dancer and an animateur, she has contributed greatly over the past thirty years to the development of Indian classical dance in Britain and throughout the wider Indian diaspora, and has been one of the leading lights on the Indian classical dance and music scene. Indeed, her work in this area has already been mentioned in books such as *Parampara – Continuing the Tradition: Thirty Years of Indian Dance and Music in Leicester,* by Colin Hyde, Smita Vadnerkar and Angela Cutting [1] and *Karman – History of South Asia Dance in the UK: With Special Reference to Leicester and Leicestershire,* by Cynthia Brown and Werner Menski. [2]

The back cover of *Parampara*, published to commemorate 30 years of Indian dance and music in Leicester, summarises the importance of the city for the development of Indian dance in Britain thus:

> Dance has long been an important part of the cultural and religious life of the people of the Indian sub-continent, reflecting a rich variety of traditions dating back more than 3000 years. For the early small groupings of Indians who settled in Leicester in the 1950s and 60s, opportunities to take part in traditional dance and music events were few indeed. However, thanks to the enthusiasm and initiative of individuals and organisations within the local community, Leicester has now become one of the leading centres for Indian dance and music in Britain.

Leicester is a multi-ethnic, multi-faith city, with a population of over a third of a million, and is home to a large immigrant population, which includes communities from South Asia, the Caribbean and Europe. According to the National Census of 2011, 163,203 people, or 49.9 % of the total population of the city were from ethnic minorities. 93,335 of these individuals (28.3 %) were of Indian descent. Meanwhile, Christians now make up less than a third of the population (106,872 people [32.4 %]). The total numbers of Muslims (61,440 people [18.6%]), Hindus (50,087 people [15.2 %]) and Sikhs (14,457 people [4.4 %]) account for 38.2 % of the population of Leicester, the larger two groups each exceeding the number who class themselves as Christians. In term of religious affiliation, Hindus are now second only in numbers to Muslims (notably in the 2001 National Census, Hindus were the majority). [3] One of the main characteristics of Leicester, which differentiates it from many other British cities, is the fact that Indians, and Hindus in particular (including those who arrived in Britain via East Africa) have flourished in every aspect of civic life – in politics, economy, society and culture, and that they have made significant contributions to the development of the city. [4]

For instance, Belgrave Road and Melton Road, which are home to many people of Indian descent, have the appearance of Indian residential areas. They are sometimes referred to as 'Mini-Gujarat' and are now known and officially signposted as 'the Golden Mile'. Celebrations for the Hindu festival of Diwali are centred around this area, and are held on a massive scale, featuring around 6,000 Diwali lights. This event has happened around the end of October or the beginning of November every year since 1983. The festival continues for several weeks, and incorporates the nine days of Navratri, which occur before Diwali itself. It is celebrated in homes, schools, work places, Hindu temples, halls, community centres, libraries, open stages in public parks, and other venues. During this festival, tens of thousands of people from all over Britain and also from other countries visit Leicester, and throng the Melton Road, which features as the central focus of the festival. [5]

However, such high-profile celebrations, renowned throughout the Indian diaspora, would have been impossible to stage without the pioneering efforts of Indian dance teachers such as Mrs Nilima Devi, who have quietly nurtured their art in the city over the years. Indian dance and music are indispensable to such festivals, and they have lent much of the 'glamour' to these events. Dance and music are an integral part of everyday life, and part of the cultural inheritance of the Indian community, and they are crucial to cultivating a sense of identity. I very much hope that this volume on Mrs Devi's life story will give a fresh insight into the history of the multi-ethnic city of Leicester, into the lives of its Indian residents, and into the Hindu community itself.

The above mentioned booklets *Parampara* and *Karman*, contain brief summaries of Mrs Devi's life story. This booklet, however, not only details her activities as an Indian classical dancer and her thoughts and philosophy on the subject of dance, but also describes her homeland, the city Vadodara in India and her family, her upbringing, marriage to Professor Werner Menski,[6] her experience of bringing up children, and her relationship to Leicester itself. In addition, Prof Menski has kindly agreed to add his own his life story to the narrative. Mr Colin Hyde,[7] who was involved in the *Parampara* project, and Mrs Cynthia Brown,[8] who was involved in the *Karman* project, have also kindly agreed to contribute their own recollections to this volume. In addition, two former students of Mrs Devi, Mrs Gita Lakhlani and Mr Aakash Odedra, himself a rising dancer, who now performs all over the world, have contributed accounts of studying with their much-respected teacher, and have contributed their own memories of their experiences in the world of Indian classical dance (both are included in the photographs which accompany the text). The inclusion of this type of material is a new departure in the 'Memory and Narrative Series', and I hope it will add to a deeper understanding of Mrs Devi's life story.

This project began one day when Mrs Cynthia Brown said to me: 'Mrs Devi is an Indian

I   Introduction

classical dance teacher and she is a very interesting person to meet, so why don't you contact her?'. I was already acquainted with Prof Menski, and I was aware that his wife was Indian, but I knew little about her. I duly contacted her and she responded without delay. Subsequently, I went to meet her in the CICD office. After that, she not only provided me with a wealth of information relating to Indian classical dance and music in Leicester, but also agreed to be interviewed; indeed, she has been wholeheartedly supportive in the writing of this booklet. In all, I interviewed her three times (12 March 2013, 21 August 2013, 10 March 2014).

The foreword to this booklet has been provided by Mr Christopher Maughan, a retired Principal Lecturer in Arts and Festivals Management, De Montfort University (DMU). He is a friend of Prof Menski and I first met him at the CICD, where he was a Board member and Trustee of the institution, when I visited to take photographs. I am very grateful to him for agreeing to contribute to the project.

Notes

1   Hyde, Colin, Vadnerkar, Smita & Cutting, Angela (eds), *Parampara – Continuing the Tradition: Thirty Years of Indian Dance and Music in Leicester*, Leicester: Leicester City Council, 1996.
2   *Karman: History of South Asian Dance in Leicester and Leicestershire*, compiled by Cynthia Brown & Werner Menski, Leicester: CICD, 2012.
3   2001 Census; 2011 Census (see p. 187, p. 191).
4   John Martin & Gurharpal Singh, *Asian Leicester*, Stroud: Sutton Publishing, 2002.
5   Sato Kiyotaka (ed.), *The Life Story of Mr Ramanbhai Barber, MBE, DL: The President of the Shree Sanatan Mandir in Leicester*, Tokyo: Research Centre for the History of Religious and Cultural Diversity (Meiji University), 2015.
6   Prof Menski is now Emeritus Professor of South Asian Laws and his publications include *Modern Indian Family Law*, Richmond: Curzon Press, 2000; *Hindu Laws: Beyond Tradition and Modernity*, New Delhi: Oxford University Press, 2003; and *Comparative Law in a Global Context: The Legal Systems of Asia and Africa*, second edition, Cambridge: Cambridge University Press, 2006.
7   Mr Colin Hyde is a researcher and outreach officer in the East Midlands Oral History Archive (EMOHA), at the Centre for Urban History at the University of Leicester. He has worked on a number of community-based oral history projects in Leicestershire and Rutland, including publications such as *Walnut Street Past, Present, Future* (1995) and *TH Wathes: A Century of Service* (2004); Book Review: 'Kiyotaka Sato, Memory and Narrative Series 1-5, Research Centre for the History of Religious and Cultural Diversity, Meiji University, Tokyo. 2010-2012', *Sundai Shigaku (Sundai Historical Review)*, no.148, March 2013, 161-170.
8   Mrs Cynthia Brown is a former project manager of the East Midlands Oral History Archive at the University of Leicester. Mrs Brown's publications include *Wharf Street Revisited*, Leicester: Leicester City Council, 1995; 'Moving on: Reflections on

Oral History and Migrant Communities in Britain', *Oral History*, vol.34, no.1, 2006; *The Story of the Saff: A History of the Saffron Lane Estate*, Leicester: Leicester City Council, 1998; *Leicester Voices*, Stroud: Tempus, 2002; 'Oral Testimony as a Historical Source: Strengths and Challenges', *Discussion Paper* [Research Centre for the History of Religious and Cultural Diversity, Meiji University, Tokyo], no.4, 2015.

II
The Life Story of Mrs Nilima Devi, MBE

II The Life Story of Mrs Nilima Devi, MBE

1 My birthplace and my family background

Mrs Nilima Devi was born in Vadodara [formerly Baroda], in the Gujarat state, India in 1953. She recalls her memories thus:

My birthplace — Vadodara,[1] Gujarat state, India

My name is Nilima Devi, and my married surname is Menski. Nilima Devi is my artistic name and most people know me as Nilima Devi. I was given this title in my first public performance in Wuppertal in Germany when I was performing for the German-Indo Society there in 1979. They made a big poster with my name as Nilima Devi. When we came to the UK I was officially Nilima Menski. As Menski did not sound like an Indian surname, people constantly asked me about my married name. I had to tell the story of our marriage because my marriage was not a love marriage, but an arranged marriage. I became quite tired of telling people my story. When we were making my professional brochure, my husband said to me: 'You should not make your name Nilima Menski, but Nilima Devi. If you do so no one would ask about your surname'. Since then, I have been using my artistic name Nilima Devi in public.

Young Nilima, 1954.

I was born on 23 July 1953 in Vadodara in Gujarat state, India. It is a large city several hours by train north of Bombay, in the north-western part of India. It is a very beautiful city with lots of different communities. There are lots of Marathi people (Maharashtrians). My family roots are from Maharashtra, more from the south. A long time back, my forefathers went to Vadodara because it was a kingdom run by a Maharashtrian ruler, the Gaekwad of Baroda. They came from a place called Phalthan in Maharashtra,[2] in which still today many members of our ancestral family, the clan of Nimbalkars, live and work. Later on lots of our people worked in the services of the palace, in the army and in administration, so even today, though this is now in the state of Gujarat, a lot of Marathis (Maharashtrians) are living in that city and we all grew up speaking several languages.

Gujarat state is a very beautiful place and I like the state very much. Even if I go to other places, I feel that Gujarat has in comparison a very rich culture and I also like Gujarati food and people's generally friendly nature. Culturally the Gujarat state is very interesting and it has a long history of artistic heritage. As there are so many different people living there, we were early on quite familiar with different cultures and variations in people's lifestyle. Because I was born and brought up there I have some kind of deep attachment to the place. Most of our family and friends are there, although there are some in Bombay, but Gujarat is everything to me. I did go to Bombay quite a lot because there are so many relatives in Bombay. When I was young, I used to go for holidays to see my cousins and my aunts, my mother's sisters and their families.

In Gujarat there are not only Gujaratis, but also lots of Marathi people are living there. There are some Sikhs, Muslims and many Sindhis[3] as well, and quite a few Parsis, people who came originally from Persia but speak Gujarati. I think if you are Gujarati and your neighbours are Marathis, they often share food. They often do cook lovely food and appreciate and share each other's culture and celebrations. Since school times, I have lots of friends from different communities and we used to socialise a lot, mixed marriages are also happening there, among Marathis, Gujaratis, Sindhis and Parsis.

My family background

I have one younger brother and one younger sister. My father was in the Social Services of Gujarat State, looking after orphaned children. As an officer of the Gujarati Government, he had a transferable job and so we moved around Guajrat a lot when I was young. My father did not have sisters. He had only one brother, but my mother had three sisters and there was a huge maternal family. Although my mother was a housewife, she was also a social worker and used to be on the Board of Directors of the Mahila Bank, the major Women's Co-operative Bank in Vadodara, which has been running since the 1970s and is still going strong now. This bank was developed to assist poor women in building up savings, opening small-scale businesses and buying properties. My mother was one of the founding members of this bank, which has more recently been recognised by the Gujarat Government as an important institution. For example, the Finance Minister has been praising the ladies behind this bank very much for the social impact that they have clearly had.

I remember my father's parents. But I don't remember my mother's parents, because they passed away when my mother was still very young. They were four sisters. My mother and her sisters were brought up by an uncle who was the doctor to the Royal Family in Vadodara. They were living in a joint family of more than 25 people together. in quite a big house in the old centre of the city. During the 1930s and 1940s, it used to be normal to live in a joint family or an extended family.

I think after 1950 it became very much more individual families or nuclear families, just with husband, wife and children. Family life in India has changed very much over time. After the independence of India in 1947 more women started getting formal education. As indicated, as my father was travelling all around Gujarat, we also had to move around with him. We settled in Vadodara when I was eleven or twelve years old. My father thought that we shouldn't move around any more because secondary education for his children would be very difficult otherwise. Vadodara was a good city to get an education. There was also a very beautiful university, called M.S. University or Maharaja Sayajirao University [the largest university in Gujarat] after the ruler, who was a patron of that university. At that time it was very popular. It still has got a good standard and is a well-

II The Life Story of Mrs Nilima Devi, MBE

known Indian university.

2 Learning Indian classical dance, and my work career

As a young girl, Nilima Devi went to schools in India, and also started to learn Indian classical dance. This is how she remembers these foundations of her lifelong career as a dance artist in Vadodara:

Schooling

I went to primary school and then to secondary school in Vadodara. In India we have a primary school system and then from eighth standard you start secondary schooling, and then you go on to college or university. My secondary school education was in schools for girls and I studied at first in a Gujarati-medium school. I and my sister studied there, but my brother studied in an English-medium school because there was a view that boys had to be educated in an English school if they wanted to move on in life. Later on I went to university and first studied Commerce, and then Kathak,[4] and all that education was in English.

Learning Indian Classical Dance

Nilima graduating with a B. Com from M.S. University, Baroda in 1972.

When I was eleven or twelve years old, still very young, I used to enjoy music and dance and used to dance, so my father sent me to school to learn dance wherever we went. In Vadodara you can only join the Music College of Maharaja Sayajirao University (M.S. University) for dance classes in the evenings for a Diploma in Dance, as a hobby, once you are twelve. So when I was twelve years old, I joined the diploma course in the Vadodara Music College and did my Diploma in Kathak there in 1969. I passed with Distinction and used to get lots of first class marks, and lots of prizes, which motivated me to study further. After the Diploma some people encouraged me to do a full degree in dance. I was studying Commerce at the same time as I was doing my dance degree, so I went to two colleges of the University. During the morning I would go and do my training in dance and in the afternoon I would go to the Commerce College and from there to the Fine Arts Department to take some other subjects related to dance. Then in the evening again, there would be some dance practice or learning of some music. So I basically did two degrees at the same time. I completed my B. Com in 1971 and after that I finished the Bachelors degree in Dance (B Mus Kathak) with another Distinction in 1973. After that I also took a Masters degree in Dance (M Mus Kathak) in 1975. I remember that a choreography course by the famous Kathak artist Maya Rao from

Bangalore in 1974 inspired me a lot.

At that time my family was quite forward-thinking in terms of female education, especially my paternal grandfather. He used to tell my father that he must educate his daughters, they must have an education. My father was a government officer and himself an educated man. He understood that education was also very important for women and thus for his girls. My father, when he was a young man, went to see a classical Indian dance performance, and very much liked it. At that time he thought he must start to educate his daughters about Indian dance as well. He decided that if he gets married and has a daughter, she should learn dance. So I was very lucky. But my mother's uncle was not so happy that I was seriously learning dance, because dance was not something that was seen as a good hobby in India at that time for girls from a respectable family. My grandfather had seen women in the palace dancing and giving drinks to kings and princes and other palace people. He thought it was that kind of dance called *nautch* dance, not a respectable occupation for an educated girl. He didn't realise that I was actually learning something very special, which has got much cultural relevance and an educational value as well. It is very difficult if people do no have that kind of awareness. Now because of TV and all that, more people seem to understand what is classical dance and classical music. But there are still lots of people who do not believe that their daughters should learn dance. I faced that same opposition later in Leicester, when some parents objected to their daughters wanting to learn dance.

My work career

After I finished the Masters in Dance I thought I would get a job in a bank, because I was not very sure that I would be able to dance after marriage because still traditional families might not allow me. They say you are married and have to look after your family and should not dance, so I was looking to work somewhere. I tried to get a job in a bank but somehow it didn't work out. I then found a job with Vadodara City Council and worked there for five or six years. In between I also started teaching dance because I thought if I can't perform I should at least be able to teach

The board on the wall of Nilima's home in Baroda, advertising 'Classical Kathak Dance Class' in Gujarati and English.

dance. So I started teaching Kathak classes. We had a large house in India and I had a big hall there, so I started teaching dance at our house in Vadodara. The pupils were all Indian girls – no boys. They were aged eight, nine and ten. Some were fifteen or sixteen. Actually, I only taught for one year, then I got married and went abroad.

II The Life Story of Mrs Nilima Devi, MBE

3 My marriage

Mrs Nilima Devi got married to a German academic in 1979. She recalls her memories thus:

My marriage

My marriage is quite a story! My future husband wanted to marry an Indian girl and he had looked at some girls in Leicester. He had been doing research on Asian shops in Leicester in 1975-6 and was a geographer who also studied English, Hindi, Sanskrit and Indian Studies. While doing his studies in Germany he came to Leicester in August 1972 to teach German to British school children. Of course summer 1972 was exactly the time when Idi Amin of Uganda threw out all Asians from his country. Many of them had relatives in Leicester and came to this particular city in the UK.[5] So my husband met many Ugandan and other East African Asians, and at that time he also came in touch with some Indian teachers, and was introduced to a Panjabi Asian family that taught him much about Indian culture the Sachdeva family.

Some years later, he conducted field research on Asian shops in Leicester for his MA thesis in Germany. As a result, he talked to many more Indians and learnt more about their culture and their migration history and so on. I think at that time something clicked with him that he would be very happy if he married an Indian girl. He liked Indian culture very much. People welcomed him, fed him because he used to speak Hindi and liked him because he could communicate in various languages. He can also understand Gujarati a little, but he cannot speak it fluently. He speaks Hindi very well, in fact extremely well. He also writes it very well. At that time, some of his friends showed him some British Asian girls, but mostly he didn't like them because they wanted to become more Western through marrying a European guy. He liked one or two girls, but the parents were not happy, because they had only one daughter and didn't want to give her to a foreigner.

I think my father was at first not very happy that I should get in contact with a foreigner, because I am the eldest. I also have a brother and a younger sister. He was not happy that being a Hindu girl, I was marrying a Christian, although my husband is more Hindu than anything else. Of course we had an arranged marriage. My grandfather always believed in astrology and horoscopes. When we were born, horoscopes were made for all of us. After my birth, he told my father that my horoscope was special and he also told him that for the first daughter, he had to match the horoscope to get her happily married. So my father used to look for many boys in India, but the horoscopes were not matching. And then, if it did match to some extent, he said there was a slight problem, but you might try fasting after marriage on certain days of the week. I said: 'I am not going to do fasting for marriage, because if it is not matching properly, why should I get married to that man in the first place? I want a perfect match'. I remember that my father used to get quite angry as I got older and refused all proposals.

II The Life Story of Mrs Nilima Devi, MBE

My husband was of course still living in Germany and studying there. He had met one musician from Baroda in Germany, because he used to go and see Indian dance and music performances there, so he gave his card to some artists. One day, this musician found himself stranded in Germany and asked my future husband for help. He was from Vadodara, had also studied Kathak dance at the Baroda Music College where I was studying Kathak, but he was mainly a tabla and santoor player. His father was a music teacher at that College, and the family used to live near to our house. So the musician and my future husband became good friends and this man helped him in looking for a suitable girl. In late 1978, the Indian artist wrote to his father in Vadodara, and his father then came to our house and said that there was a German man who wants to marry an Indian girl.

We didn't pay any attention to him because I said there are lots of girls in your class, why don't you ask them? I thought that it was very difficult to marry a foreigner and to marry a European was a frightening thought. A lot of divorces were happening. I thought that girls who couldn't get married might think about this. He said no, they want a smart girl like you. I said that it was very difficult. Nothing happened for some time because the music teacher couldn't find any girls. The music teacher's son said that after he had written to his father, he was not taking it seriously and therefore suggested to this German man to write directly to the father, especially as they were planning to go to India anyway. He therefore advised this young German to write to his father in Baroda, if possible in Hindi, and to explain his motives. So he wrote about his ideas of what kind of girl he wanted to this music teacher, who got very excited seeing this long letter, largely written in Hindi. He came to us saying that this man has written again, and we should come to his house and see the letter. I didn't pay any attention because I thought why should one bother?

Then one day there was a strike in the music college. I was coming home and the music teacher was walking behind me. He asked me if I could go to his house and look at the photographs. Did I have time? I went to his house and looked at the photographs and the way that this young German had written was indeed fascinating. His handwriting was beautiful. I couldn't believe that a German person was writing like this in Hindi. The way he expressed himself was so beautiful, too. I began to think that I should have the sort of person who thinks like that. You don't just get married to cook and clean in the house, but you can also do a lot of other work as well – for instance you can keep up your profession. His photographs looked good, too, so the music teacher said why don't you try for yourself? I said I couldn't, because first of all I had to find out if my horoscope matched or not. If my stars matched with his, then maybe we could think about it.

That is how the ball started rolling. The German man did not have a horoscope, so we asked him to send the time of his birth, the date and the place where he was born. My father went to our family astrologer who made a horoscope for the two of us, and to our surprise the astrologer said to my father that this was the best horoscope so far for your daughter! My father could not believe this and asked the astrologer to double-check, but

II The Life Story of Mrs Nilima Devi, MBE

Nilima in Baroda in 1978.

Nikima in Baroda in 1978.

the same result was given. I think this gave my family some courage to allow me to meet this German man after he came to India in February 1979. Because he spoke Hindi, we could communicate easily. He spoke softly, ate all Indian food, and I didn't find him to be a foreigner – I thought he was from northern India and maybe from Kashmir. He looked like a Kashmiri man. He loved Indian culture and spoke beautiful Hindi. He really impressed me. I felt that our Indian young people don't even speak Hindi very well, but somebody from outside our culture can speak it. So I didn't find him to be a foreigner when he came to India.

Nilima in Baroda, March 1979.

We then had some discussions over two weeks and got engaged in early March. We got married very soon, on 9 May 1979 and had a Hindu wedding ceremony in Baroda. In Germany we later only had a reception. We have lovely photographs of the wedding. My husband's parents couldn't come, but his Hindi teacher from Bombay, Professor Jagdish Chandra Jain, was present. My husband had thought that his mother would come, but the month of May is very hot in India and anyway everything was done in a rush. My horoscope had said that I must get married before a certain time of the year. If I married after 1979 it would be very difficult. So we had to rush! It was crazy!

Hindu wedding ceremony [6]

A Hindu wedding ceremony involves many different rituals over several days. One puts Henna (*mehndi*) on the hands of the bride and there are purificatory rituals with turmeric paste and many other preparations and blessings. Then the bride is brought to the wedding hall by her maternal uncles and the main wedding rituals start. There are rituals of the first holding of hands, the singing of poetic wedding songs and blessings (*mangalashtaka*) and mutual garlanding of the parties. Later rituals are done in front of a fire as the divine witness. We both sit together, husband and wife, and the priest chants some verses (*shlokas*) and we perform more rituals. One offers homage to the fire by giving it butter (*ghi*), water, rice and flowers. Normally it takes hours to complete these wedding rituals. At some point the couple will need to go round the fire, four times clockwise, to make an oath or contract that they are going to be together forever. In many cases, the bride then finally also walks on seven heaps of rice, which binds the parties together as friends for life. Because this marriage ceremony is very important, you feel very happy. But at the same time you have to leave your parents' house, so you also feel very sad, it's a mixed feeling. At the end, husband and wife feed each other sweets and then many more pictures are taken, with relatives and friends and guests at the wedding. We had an evening reception, with many more pictures, and then just a few days later I went with my husband, who had to resume his job, straight to Germany. At that time, it was a little easier than today to get a spouse visa.

4 Moving to Germany, and my life in Germany

After her marriage in 1979 Mrs Nilima Devi went to Germany with her husband to live there. They lived there for about one year. She remembers her life there thus.

Nilima and Werner in Bochum, Germany, May 1979.

We lived in the city of Bochum (a city in the state of North Rhine-Westphalia) in central Germany for around eighteen months. We lived in a nice flat in the centre of the town near a big park with a lake and beautiful flowers and I had my first son there. He was born in Germany because we were basically waiting for him to be born there, as I had a very good doctor there, and then we moved to Leicester soon after that. I had difficulty living in Germany. It was quite shocking. My husband had said that life is very different in Europe, but of course I didn't realise what the real situation would be. Life is so very different in India and especially everything is much more open. The windows and doors are open, people come and go, and it is not isolated like in Europe. It was a very different experience and I felt very homesick and wanted to go back to India. My husband understood and said that he really loved India and he would like to do his PhD in India, but we could not go at that time. After our marriage we would stay in Germany for one year and then perhaps we could go to India. He could pursue his PhD there on a German government scholarship, and he said maybe he might like to live in India forever. It was a question of one year only and then we were going to be in India. After seeing India, though, I think he understood that India was not the right place for him. He was not sure whether he would settle in India or not, because there are lots of people who can teach Hindi there, and he was also afraid that if we went to India we would never come back to Europe.

II The Life Story of Mrs Nilima Devi, MBE

Fortunately, there were some Indians in the city of Bochum in Germany, and especially my doctor's family was a massive help. Doctor Amin was from Vadodara as well, so that is how we got in touch. Dr. (Mrs.) Amin, a Parsi lady, insisted that I should have my baby in Bochum under her expert supervision. There were also some Indian students at the university and they became friends. I think what happened was that slowly I started preparing for my performances in Germany, despite the pregnancy, and then we invited a tabla player over from India to perform with me. I gave several performances in Germany with him and later also danced to taped music.

I was expecting a baby, and so I started settling down and was busy. The first few months were really difficult when I was new in Germany and then slowly I started liking it. Everything was such a culture shock, because you come from India, and suddenly you don't see the sun, so you feel a lot of depression. You are all the time in the house and most people speak in German. My husband would go to the university and could only come back in the evening. I was alone in the house, a completely new experience. I didn't know German but learnt a bit in Germany, going to some classes as well. I actually found the German language very difficult. I didn't like the sound and found it harsh. My husband said: 'Don't think in an Indian language, don't think in English, only think in German'! That was very difficult to follow. That is not how we learn a language in India – that you forget your own language and think in another. You learn it naturally. It is a natural process of learning.

5   Moving to England and to Leicester

As Nilima's husband changed his scholarship from India to England, they went to Leicester in September 1980. She recalls her new life thus:

I went to Germany in early May 1979 and around the end of June that year, we both came to Britain for the first time for a week or ten days and met my husband's friends. We then went back to Germany. So I saw England before we settled in Leicester and he showed me the house that we had there. At that time I didn't like England and thought Germany was much cleaner. I thought, my God, in India we live in big houses and the space there is very nice and the windows are always open. I found this house in England very small, with very different architecture. But because he had our own house, we ended up staying in Churchill Street, Highfields area [7] in Leicester and later simply made it a nice place.

My husband then changed his scholarship from India to England and concentrated first on completing his PhD at the School of Oriental and African Studies (SOAS) in London. When we came from Germany in September 1980 with the first little son, we started living in Leicester because my husband had bought this house in Churchill Street earlier, in 1975 while he was a student. After his PhD he was offered a full-time job at London University and simply commuted by train a few days a week. However, we resolved that we were going to stay in Leicester and made everything bigger and more comfortable. We had lots of space, even a dance studio for my own work. I started liking Leicester after that and thought that it was great.

When I came to Leicester I looked for facilities where one could teach dance, but there were no such possibilities to go and teach in Leicester. I went to some community centres, but nobody taught dance there and people did not know much about classical dance. Some Asian women from Kenya had taught for a little while and then they moved away from Leicester. Sometimes for social or cultural occasions and festivals a group of people would come together and create some dances and then they performed them. There was no sort of dance master here or an artist who taught dance properly on a consistent basis.

We had an outhouse at the back of our property which had much earlier been used for storing things and smoking sausages for the Polish butcher's shop in Leicester, which is what our house had previously been. My husband said: 'Why don't we turn this into a dance studio? There is a separate passageway here, so students can come in that way, and nobody needs to come through the house'. Soon after we came to the UK in September 1980, we made it a very comfortable space for learning dance, with the help of some friends. Then from 1 January 1981 onwards, once I had settled down, I started teaching Kathak classes in that studio.

Teaching Indian dance in English was fine. After all, I had done my university studies in English in India and this was not a problem. The only thing was that you didn't speak English in India all the time, but in the UK you did, so I learnt more spoken English. As my primary school education had been in Gujarati, it was easy for me to communicate with Leicester's many Gujarati-speaking people. I had of course learnt to speak Marathi, which is my mother tongue. I can also speak Hindi because we used to study Hindi at school. I can speak Hindi, Gujarati, Marathi and English and I can read Sanskrit.

It is good that we had our house here in Leicester, though my husband had a lecturing job in London. When I saw London I didn't like it. Leicester reminded me of my home city in India, Vadodara. Everything is close by and many people speak Gujarati or Hindi. You don't have to travel so much by car or bus. In five or ten minutes you can go from one place to another. In London you had to go by underground and there was too much travelling.

There is probably another reason why we settled in Leicester. My husband had known earlier that Leicester had quite a lot of Indian people. He had bought our house when he was still a student because at that time he thought that he might stay in England rather than in Germany. When he bought this house in 1975 it was no longer a Polish butcher's shop. A Gujarati family lived there and they wanted to open a shop but then decided to move to the Belgrave area,[8] in fact to the newly developed area of Rushey Mead, because there were more Gujarati people moving there.

II The Life Story of Mrs Nilima Devi, MBE

48-50 Chuchill Street in Leicester.

My husband had bought this house earlier thinking that he might turn it into a cultural institute to teach Hindi and Sanskrit to people in Leicester. He didn't realise, of course, that he was going to marry a dance artist who could use this place. This is how the Centre for Indian Classical Dance (CICD) [9] developed. After some years we bought the house next door, which had belonged to an Eastern European family and then we expanded our house and the dance studio in 1984 and made everything more beautiful and comfortable. I started to settle down and the boys went to Medway [Community Primary] School (in St Stephen's Road, Highfields), which is near to our house and very convenient. They first went to infants school and then primary school there. I started liking our area because I could buy Indian vegetables in the Indian shops nearby. You could find all kinds of Indian foods and vegetables, and all the pulses. I felt like I was in India, not in a foreign country.

My husband is German and has partly Polish heritage. There are certainly differences between my culture and his. He was a foreigner, but I felt that he was also part of India. He said that he was a Hindu and he doesn't go to church and that was a plus point for me. But then, once I came to Europe, I found him much more German than Indian. In Germany he was not normally wearing Indian dress. This was a big change, because in India he wore Indian dress almost all the time. Although he says that he is a Hindu, he has got a very German mentality. The way he works, and in lots of other things. He also doesn't like spending much time socially because he has so much to do academically. He was much more German than I had thought, and it was very difficult at times and was a big shock. But I think we both managed well and the challenges of bringing up our two boys in multicultural Leicester also brought us closer together and we learnt from the experiences of our children.

6 My children's education and their marriage

Mrs Nilima Devi has two sons. She recalls their education and marriage thus:

We have two children. Our eldest son was born in Germany in 1980 and our younger one was born in Leicester in 1982. Because we were both very busy with our respective professions, we did not have much space left for a social life, but we were very focused on the upbringing of our children. On several days a week, and sometimes from Monday to Friday, my husband would be in London, and at the weekend and on days when he was in Leicester he would look after them. I would take care of them at the other times, it worked well. In the beginning my mother sometimes came over from India, so when the boys were six or seven years old, I could start part-time dance work but was still much in the house and was not yet working full-time outside the house, focusing more on dance classes in the studio. When they began going to school full-time, I started doing more education work outside and also some community work. Once they were nine or ten years old they managed much better by themselves and did not need to be picked up from school, for example. I also taught them dance and music, so they were with me most of the time. They never felt bored, as there was always something to do.

Whenever I was performing more intensively and touring, my mother would come from India to look after the boys. This was because I didn't want my children to be looked after by other people who did not know them. Sometimes I had to stay somewhere else overnight and didn't want any strange persons living in the house looking after the children. I was so lucky that my mother could come from India. My husband initially wanted some kind of au pair girl to look after the boys, so we had some au pairs from Italy and Germany. But I didn't like them because either they were smoking, or would wear strange clothes and they were always on the phone. I told my husband that I didn't trust them to look after the children well enough. It would be better if my mother came, so they could learn to be with their grandmother and they would have that kind of close, family-based relationship. When my mother was here I also didn't have to worry because she would feed them well. She would look after them and everything would be wonderful. It would be expensive anyway if you had an au pair girl. I thought why not spend that money on an air ticket for my mother? That is how we arranged it. My mother was ready to come, so why not? It was indeed much better and I didn't have to worry at all. If I was out of Leicester, my mother would look after the kids, and I would bring everything for her that she needed to cook. The children were very happy with their grandmother. Like my husband, I didn't have any family here in the UK, so it was somewhat difficult. Bringing my mother here as a family person was very helpful both mentally and emotionally as well. Your children are in safe hands.

My children went to Medway [Community Primary] School in Highfields. I have been there several times, also to do some dance workshops. By the time we came to the UK and our children went to school, multicultural and multi-faith education had already started. It developed more strongly in the 1970s and made sense in a place like Leicester. I believe multicultural education in the UK and certainly in cities like Leicester is very important. My children really enjoyed studying in this kind of environment because they also experienced that living diversity in our home. Through school and their friends from school they also came to learn about other people, their faiths and languages, about various types of black community, Muslim, Hindu, Sikh and Jain communities, Gujaratis, Panjabis and others. I think it is very important to get young people, especially, to appreciate different cultures and religions. Of course they also learnt about English culture, but the schools they went to were really very multicultural and certainly not just an English educational environment. Some of the teachers were really excellent at cultivating a sense of cultural pluralism, others were not so keen.

II The Life Story of Mrs Nilima Devi, MBE

If you educate your children well, they will become more broad-minded, and I think one faces less problems, otherwise it is sometimes not nice. Our older son faced some racism early on in school, and in response we sent both boys for karate lessons. Nobody ever touched them again! We also had some further trouble with languages. We spoke so many languages in our two families that the children rebelled at some point and said they were getting confused, could we please stick to English? We could see the problem. When we went to Germany, it was their grandparents' local dialect there and not only German. When they went to India, it was Marathi at home, Gujarati on the streets and with neighbours and friends, and then much Hindi, too. As my husband and I spoke Hindi most of the time in the house, the boys needed to know Hindi, too. We agreed at some point that we had better focus on one language properly first, namely English, rather than mixing so many languages. Of course children learn language very fast and quite easily. I remember that when the older one was about four years old, I went with the kids to India for several months. The older one came back fluent in Marathi, and had forgotten all his English. Within a few weeks, however, it seems that he had forgotten all his Marathi and was fluent again in English. So they had a lot of practice in different languages. When they were seven or eight years old, I tried to take them to local Hindi teachers and we also taught them the Hindi alphabet. When they were ten or eleven years old, this kind of extra study became too much, however, because they were also doing Indian dance, ballet and music lessons, and some other activities. Once they went to secondary school, we had to stop learning Hindi because their whole timetable changed and involved too much work. When they went to secondary school, first Judgemeadow [Community College], (Marydene Drive, Evington) and then for 'A' levels to [Wyggeston and] Queen Elizabeth I College (University Road), they also had much homework. But throughout they carried on learning Indian dance, music and ballet.

By the time they completed their 'A' levels, they also stopped their training in music and dance, the latter after completing their Diploma in Kathak. We had insisted that our sons should study German and French for their 'A' levels and they both took Geography as well. They did not want to become scientists or doctors, that was clear. Our older son then moved on to take a joint degree in Hindi/Urdu, South Asian Studies and Geography at SOAS in London. He likes learning languages, and soon spoke and wrote Hindi very well, because he had excellent teachers there and also he could fall back on earlier knowledge and skills. He also studied Brazilian Portuguese and later went to India for fieldwork for his doctoral thesis, making good use of his Indian language skills. He loves talking to people in different languages and is now learning Spanish because he works in America. Our younger one claims he is not so much a language person. He went on to study law and social anthropology at the LSE (London School of Economics), where he also learnt Spanish, however. Meanwhile he has been working for several years in Japan and now knows that language, too. He also speaks some Hindi, and certainly understands a lot, but functions mainly in English.

Both our sons, as lawyers with global law firms, acknowledge that it helps them in their work that they have had such an intercultural background. Our eldest one got married a few years back to a woman who is half American and half German but grew up in China and is fluent in Mandarin. We are becoming even more diverse. She likes India very much, has been to India many times, and intriguingly her maternal grandparents lived in India for 53 years and worked there as development advisors even during colonial times. She remembers visiting them in India as a young child. She is also a lawyer and the young couple now live and work in Washington DC. For them, Leicester has become a small village, a place that they may visit to take some rest, maybe, but no longer home.

I agreed when they said they wanted to get married. The thing is that times have changed now. You must follow, otherwise… no chance! I would have liked my sons to marry Indian girls, but they feel that they were brought up here and being half Indian and half German, they prefer someone of a mixed or different background. The whole concept of marriage has changed. Before in India, a son used to get married to bring home a wife who could look after the family. Now they mainly see themselves and are two individuals who want to be together. They will look after the family, but are not staying with the family. They are adults and make their own choice. Parents are no longer that important. They don't want an arranged marriage according to Indian culture because they say: 'You didn't marry like that, so why are you telling us?'. They don't quite understand that mine was a unique marriage, arranged largely because of the horoscopes. They also can't quite believe how I lived in India and then in Germany. They find it intriguing, but also almost unbelievable. None of their friends could believe it was really like that. Times have really changed.

I also think that the caste system, if there ever was one, is coming apart. It used to be very strong in terms of identity. People wanted that the boy and girl married within their own caste, but nowadays it is rather different. People are thinking outside the box. Some families, especially Hindu families, are quite liberal. But arranged marriages are still happening, too, though not the way it used to be. Nowadays often the boy and girl find each other and then the parents agree. Love marriages are happening more and more these days, as boys and girls go out together and it is no longer such a taboo. Nowadays people go to discos or to see films, and they go to restaurants and often meet when they are studying at university or through work. They find their own match, and then they talk to their parents. The parents talk to each other's family, and if the match is good and they both really like each other, then a 'love marriage' can take place.

I think my sons feel that they are global citizens. They are really international and do not belong to any one community. They really feel that they are international. Of course they are also Indian, and they know that by birth they are both German and Indian. There are not many Maharashtrian Germans. Since my youngest son was born and brought up here, he is actually a British citizen by birth. The elder one was born in Germany and came here as a one month old baby on a German passport. Meanwhile he has also become British, and through marriage to an American also has a Green Card now. Both our sons have, through me as their mother, the status of Overseas Citizens of India, which means they have a permanent visa for India. They travel a lot and this probably adds to the feeling that they are global citizens and that Leicester is just a small dot on the world map. It remains part of their own history, but is no longer of much direct relevance, though life in the city shaped their identity and partly makes them who they are today.

7   Teaching Indian classical dance in Leicester

Mrs Nilima Devi started teaching in Leicester in 1981. She recalls her memories thus:

Teaching Indian classical dance

I started teaching at my studio in 1981 and began with three students. Then soon hundreds of women and young people wanted to learn dance. They would come and learn for a little while and then they would leave, because some people found it difficult and some people thought that within two weeks they would be able to learn dance and perform on stage. They didn't realise that this was classical Indian dance, and you need to have a good foundation before you will be able to perform. You have to learn the technique. You have to learn the language of the dance, so to say, the movement sequences and dance compositions and all that. It is like learning a language. You learn drama and you learn to use expressive skills along with the technique, basically you have to learn a lot of different things about dance to be able to perform it well. Since it was not easy, many people would drop out and another new group would start and then go, and then from one class there would be two-three people left, some more from another class and you combine them and move on.

We developed a structured training programme with a Kathak Diploma course, modelled at first on what I had been studying in India. I thought that I would take Vadodara Music College as my model. I looked at the diploma course from there and said OK, in India I used to go every day, here they come once a week. This will not be good enough. So I started classes twice a week and then after 4-5 months some women thought that twice a week was too much and asked if they could come only once a week. This is what we did, though it slowed everything down. We also introduced regular exams in dance. I thought if I gave them a formal syllabus, a three year syllabus at first, later six years, we could establish a full Diploma. People who had a passion for learning Kathak dance now saw that they are progressing from one year to another. They can take an exam and get a certificate. I think that gave some women and young people more inspiration to carry on. They knew that in the first year they would learn this, in the second year they would learn that, and in the third year they would learn something else. It was a real progression and we taught this Diploma for many years and it created some consistency. Altogether nine students finished the full set of six years of Kathak Diploma course.

Then in 1984, the funding bodies in the region and the Arts Council wanted that something should happen for Indian dance in the community in Leicester. So they offered me a project on Indian dance development, and I became Leicester's first Asian Dance Animateur. Leicester City Council and Leicestershire County Council supported this project jointly to raise awareness about different art forms and Indian dance styles and to teach people, demonstrate dances and give performances all over the city and county. I went around to hundreds of schools over the years, and seem to know almost every village school in the county. At first, there were no other teachers of Indian dance forms. I was the only one in Leicester, one artist for Indian dance teaching for many years.

Soon there were some 25-30 people learning Kathak dance seriously in my studio. In addition, as the Asian Dance Animateur,[10] I also used to go and demonstrate and teach dance in schools and communities, because people did not have to pay me. My fee was coming from the City Council and the County Council, and this worked well. Looking back, that was another problem, namely people don't like to pay for learning dance. They want to learn, but for free! Working as a Dance Animateur was a wonderful arrangement, as I did not have to ask people to pay money. You just go and dance and teach. In this way, I visited hundreds of schools and colleges and familiarised thousands of people with Indian dance. Then, gradually, lots of community centres wanted to teach dance. I couldn't do this all myself, as I had two children and it was simply too much. Soon some women who were training in dance at my centre showed interest in becoming dance tutors. So I trained them to become dance teachers, and some of them were already trained teachers, which helped a lot. We developed special skills-based programmes and established a tailor-made training course for them. I invited some professional musicians and other dance artists to come and teach them so that they could learn new things. They learnt how music is relating to dance, how dance is taught systematically, how to take a class, and how to teach and plan lessons. In this way we taught many women and some of them became very active dance teachers themselves. I taught not only in Leicester, but also in Nottingham, where I started in 1982 and offered classes until 1986/87. Some of those women also started learning more dance in Leicester later, so they were all deeply involved in this Indian/Asian dance development project and learnt how to teach dance at various levels. I trained many teachers in this way and many are still working in the various centres and some are also offering classes and tuition in Nottingham, Derby, Loughborough, London and elsewhere. Some of my best students have moved abroad and are now teaching dance in various parts of America, Italy and elsewhere.

As part of the project we used to have showcases at all the big theatres in Leicester. We used to teach various sorts of dance, not only Indian classical dance. Many pupils also learnt different Indian folk dances and all sorts of dancing. As part of the project, we also provided them some teachers from elsewhere to come and teach unusual or new dance forms which students would learn about and then perform in a showcase event. Like this, for ten years there were quite a number of people who learnt different dance styles and we created massive productions that attracted full-house audiences. During that period things changed a lot. When I had first started in 1981, there was a real hunger of people to learn Indian classical dance and various folk dance forms. After 1985 and until 1991 I was out teaching and preparing shows for the Asian Dance Animateur Project and we now reached tens of thousands of people.

Then in 1991, Leicester City Council said that they would like somebody to start working as a Dance Development Officer and the County Council wanted me to become an Advisory Teacher for Indian Dance. So I worked for both the City and County Councils in those capacities for more than ten years. We started to train still more people to teach Indian dance forms, and my own centre in Churchill Street now became a hub for those people who wanted to become artists and dancers. They would only come here to train at advanced levels. I didn't take many beginners here, since all the younger children and beginners were learning at various educational centres in Leicester and Leicestershire. This was convenient as many people didn't have to travel and make extra journeys, as some people didn't have private transport. Apart from school-based dance training projects, the Knighton Fields Dance and Drama Centre became for many years a very special centre for solid education in Indian dance and music. This was only possible because of sustained public funding and a lot of input from a dedicated team of dance and music teachers. We did lots of projects and presented many memorable annual showcase productions. There were also numerous community productions. There was much integrated education work, where school children would learn about certain topics such as religion or storytelling, the language of dance, geography and even musical mathematics. Gifted young people were selected from schools all over the city and county to learn Indian classical dance systematically. They were soon performing as part of the County Council's education system, at summer festivals, at the Easter Gala. They also used to perform at Christmas when we did an annual Christmas show at De Montfort Hall. So as part of mainstream dance education we used to offer Indian dance. I have lots of videos from that time. That was a peak time for the multicultural education system and the community. All of this collapsed when changes in government funding structures led to the withdrawal of public funding and people were expected to pay for these services. This was not sustainable and by 2010 the Knighton Fields Dance and Drama Centre closed, while music education continued.

Meanwhile I obtained some government funding to develop after-school activities and classes. We also got organisational and development money to set up a larger office. For some time, we had several staff members working for Indian dance as well, but then this also declined through lack of funding. It was quite difficult for me to carry on because there was no one person working to look at the whole picture and we now had to spend a lot of time on fundraising, as direct local authority support was more and more reduced and finally stopped. I put in a lot of my own money to carry on with this work over the years. We used to have our own community dance showcases as well. We used to get lots of offers to go and perform here and there and I involved lots of groups in such performances. Some groups even went to Scotland, taking part in the Edinburgh

Fringe Festival already in 1989. Later we went to Ireland and Italy as well, and of course we performed in a lot of places all over the UK. In 2002, I went to Japan and performed there.

I used to do my own productions with my own dance company as well, and we also performed a lot for and with them. I took some of my best dancers for auditions to national and international competitions. One major collaborative work was *The Ugly Duckling*. Many school groups worked with me and my students in this theatre production, which we turned into a full Indian dance drama, based on the famous story by Hans Christian Andersen. It is the story of how that so-called ugly duckling turns into a beautiful swan. We involved a lot of school children as farmyard animals, and groups of my junior and senior Kathak students became the little duckling, the ducks on the pond, the dogs, the cat and the old lady, and of course our star students became the Ugly Duckling. At that time we had a lot of well-trained older girls of 18-19+ who became the beautiful swans of the drama's finale. It was wonderfully set to a special Indian music score and many people remember this particular set of performances. My own children were also dancing in this production and were one of the dogs and the cat.

We have certainly done a lot of showcases in the past, but after more than 30 years of this activity and following our 30-year celebrations in 2011, I am not sure if I want to arrange any big showcases of this kind again. But we have an extensive archive and many videos from that wonderful time in the history of multicultural dance development in Leicester and Leicestershire.

My visits to Japan

The first time I went to visit Japan was in 2002. My husband was a Visiting Professor at the Tokyo University of Foreign Studies during that year. So I and the boys went to see him there, and then we all travelled to Osaka. I had established contact with an Indian dancer there, Nalini Toshniwal, and performed for her institution in Osaka and Kobe and then conducted some Kathak workshops for her students. The year after, I developed further links through a travelling grant from the Sasakawa Foundation to establish a community relationship project between Japan and the UK. I went to Osaka and Kobe again and also to Kyoto, co-operating with Nalini and her students there. We prepared some dance pieces together for an evening performance in Kyoto. We also worked with a wonderful traditional Japanese dancer and created a story-telling project together. Later in Tokyo, Nalini and I provided a workshop at the Tokyo University of Foreign Studies for their international students. This visit was in December 2003 and went on for three weeks.

In the following year, a whole group of Nalini's Japanese Kathak students came to Leicester and we conducted several workshops and training sessions together and presented a number of performances. I have been back to Japan since then, because our younger son has been working in Tokyo, but I did not perform on those occasions.

II The Life Story of Mrs Nilima Devi, MBE

8 Nilima Devi's MBE

Mrs Nilima Devi was awarded the MBE in 2013 and talks about her experiences and reactions thus:

Nilima displaying her MBE, 2013.

In the Queen's New Year's Honours List of 2013, I was awarded an MBE for my long-time services to dance and am of course very happy and proud about that. Several people in Britain, mainly in Leicester, must have worked behind the scenes to recommend me. It seems that this national award sparked off some movement to ensure that other Indian dancers also obtained more prominent public recognition, and that has indeed happened since. We were especially pleased that the Akademi in London, a major national South Asian dance organisation (www.akademi.co.uk), marked my award with a lunchtime celebration in London after I received the MBE at Buckingham Palace on 7 June 2013.

That day was quite special, as my husband drove me, our CICD Trustee Chris Maughan and his wife Paula to the Palace. Entering the royal courtyard in your own car and parking in the central space there in a well-organised manner was quite an experience, too. The whole ceremony on the day was meticulously planned and proceeded like clockwork, with many happy recipients and their excited families and friends. I was a bit surprised about being the only Asian to be given an award that day, and also there were very few other non-white people among the festive crowd.

The investiture ceremony itself was wonderful and truly memorable. I wore a special silk saree that had belonged to my mother. It provided a colourful contrast to the more sober shades worn by most of the other participants. Walking up to HRH Prince Charles, who acted as the Queen's representative on the day, was a very special moment. Prince Charles gave me a warm welcome. He told me that he had watched many Indian classical dance performances and was keen to know whether I would continue with my work for dance. Before you can blink, however, this moment is over, and then there was of course ample time for photographs and portraits.

It is surely important that the various achievements and contributions of Asians are acknowledged in Britain. I am especially happy that I was able to put Leicester on the national map on this occasion, too. We celebrated the 30th anniversary of CICD and my MBE award in a big function in the City Rooms of Leicester on 23 July 2013, which was also my birthday. We now need to ensure that the next generation's South Asian work is equally recognised, acknowledged and supported in all possible ways, whether private or public, and ideally in private-public partnerships, which were so very crucial to putting South Asian dance development on a stronger footing during the last decade of the twentieth century. As we are moving on, a new generation of young dancers is beginning to make a mark. I am of course especially proud of Aakash Odedra, our young rising star from Leicester, but also appreciate the efforts of many others who continue to work on various forms of Asian dance development locally, nationally and internationally. Looking back, over decades I tried to generate interest and commitment and it is increasingly recognised these days that without such efforts, Leicester would not be the vibrant multicultural place it has become and remains today, with a much higher presence and visibility of Asian and intercultural events than before in the major theatres of the city, and especially in public spaces such as the switching on of the Diwali Lights on Leicester's Golden Mile every autumn.

9 Systematic education in Indian classical dance and musical instruments

Mrs Nilima Devi explains systematic education in Indian classical dance and various musical instruments thus:

Systematic education in Indian classical dance

Ideally I think one should start classical Indian dance education at the age of six or seven. It is like learning ballet. Now of course some parents want their daughters to start from the age of three, but I don't teach such very young people. I used to teach 6+ and 7+. Now I prefer teaching advanced students and I only accept them if they want to undergo serious training in classical dance. I myself started regular Kathak dance training at the age of twelve because one couldn't join the Baroda Music College before that age. You can of course start at the age of seven or so, and I think one is never too young or too old to learn classical dance. I have got the wonderful example of one English lady from Nottingham, Joy Foxley, a trained primary school teacher, who started learning Kathak from me at the age of 45 and then went to India for the first time for her 50th birthday celebrations and to learn some more Kathak in Baroda. She still continues to learn Kathak now and also teaches others. Meanwhile she is 82, but still comes for classes, clearly for her own well-being and interest. She is also a well-versed English folk dancer. In fact her whole family is very musical. Her example certainly shows that it is never too late to start systematic education in Indian classical dance.

The musical instruments

The musical instruments are very important in Kathak dance because they provide the rhythm and melodious sound. Music is the life of Indian classical dance. In Kathak we have normally got a tabla player who plays the time cycle or 'beat' and provides rhythmic improvisation to the dancer. He also plays the intricate compositions for which Kathak dance is famous, and not all tabla players can do that or are willing to be an accompanist

II The Life Story of Mrs Nilima Devi, MBE

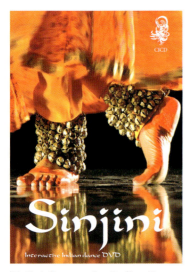

Sinjini (Interactive Indian Dance DVD), 2005.

to a dancer. Then we often have got sitar and harmonium as accompanying instruments, as well as vocal singing. All these instruments provide the time cycle according to a specific rhythm. The orchestra keeps on playing and the interaction between the accompanists and the dancer is very important. They all need to start on the first beat of a specific rhythm and finish again on the first beat of this rhythmic time cycle. Sometimes they go through two, three or four time cycles before one gets to the finish. If this is done well, people will appreciate the artists' skills and will clap spontaneously. Many people, especially in India, somehow know the traditional system and they really appreciate a good performance. In Kathak we use north Indian instruments, the tabla, the sitar, harmonium and sarod, and quite often a flute. The violin is not a north Indian instrument. It is often used in South Indian dance styles such as Bharatnatyam, however, which also uses the flute.

A Kathak dancer wears special types of clothing. We sometimes have a Hindu costume with a long skirt, a blouse and a tunic, and sometimes we have a kind of Mughal costume, where the dancer wears long trousers underneath and a long frock with lots of pleats. This change of style occurred because in later times dance performances were presented at royal courts of Hindus and Muslims. A lot of dance technique was developed for this kind of 'court dance', which presents more abstract dance compositions with intricate rhythmic patterns rather than telling old Hindu mythological and religious stories. Kathak dance is not all about stories and religious 'tradition', it also gives a lot of emphasis to highly sophisticated 'technical' dance items in which precision, clarity and speed of movements create highly artistic patterns that people can simply enjoy.

10 Hindu festivals and the history of Indian classical Kathak dance

Mrs Nilima Devi explains the relationship between Hindu festivals and the history of Indian classical dance thus:

The Hindu calendar has a lot of festivals, such as Navratri [11] and Diwali. [12] These festivals are very important also here in the UK because it is a community celebration. Among Gujaratis, the Navratri festival is organised in praise of goddess Amba. People dance certain Gujarati folk dances for nine nights around her statue and conduct beautiful rituals for her. Nowadays this is celebrated also outside India and Asians in Leicester have a long tradition of celebrating this festival in their own community centres. Some people hire a big hall and they invite well-known musicians from India. There are quite a few musicians in Britain, too, so they play music together as part of their cultural and religious celebrations. Some people fast for these nine days. The day after Navratri is called Dashera ('the tenth day'), the auspicious day when the ten-headed demon Ravana, who abducted Sita, was killed by the heroic Rama. This whole celebration, connected to the ancient stories of the epic Ramayana, commemorates the return of Rama and Sita from their exile in the forest, and the killing of the demon symbolises the victory of good over evil.

We also perform and dance the story of Rama in Indian classical dance. The Kathak style of dance developed as a form of storytelling in temples and they used to tell many stories from the ancient Indian epics, the Ramayana with the stories of Rama and Sita, the Mahabharata, and later related devotional stories about Krishna and Radha. This dance form of Kathak, which itself means 'story telling', was used to teach people about good and evil in the form of stories. Gradually, the artists started using more mime and expressions, so this became a more stylised and formalised type of dance. They also incorporated music as well to teach and entertain people, because this kind of presentation originates in an oral culture where common people couldn't read these epics. Stories needed to be told or performed. The ancient texts were either in Sanskrit or in a special medieval language, called Brajbhasha. The Kathakars, the early practitioners of Kathak, used to dance such stories to teach people about morals. That is how Kathak began, we think. After all, it means 'to tell a story'.

In India lots of historical upheavals happened especially in northern India when invaders came and ruled over centuries. Since the eleventh century Muslim rulers have been dominating most of the northern parts of India. At that time, dance artists used to perform ancient stories and religious mythology in temples which were beautiful centres of learning, a place for religious worship and discourse as well as a centre for learning various art forms, such as visual arts, dance and music. After the Muslims destroyed much of this, where would these musicians and dancers go? Many took shelter in various royal courts, where they were given protection and the chance to carry on their work and to create new work, also in classical dance. They developed a lot of new techniques and both in Hindu and Muslim royal courts, Kathak became a technically sophisticated and often aesthetically wonderful presentation of dance. There were many highly skilled dancers, musicians and teachers, they did nothing else all the time and were completely focused on their art forms. In the beginning, there were only male dancers performing in Kathak. Some Muslim kings respected and enjoyed watching Hindu stories and traditional classical dance and some even learnt to dance themselves. Many rulers were not interested in religious themes and morality lessons, however, they wanted entertainment and so they brought more female dancers to the courts. That is one of the reasons why the social reputation of dance and of dancers declined, and many middle class families do not want their daughters to learn dance even as a hobby.

I have always felt that knowing how to dance Kathak is something very special. You have to know a lot, the story and the music, and the intricate rhythmic patterns that are performed by the artist. You must know how to dance in different rhythms and then you really enjoy your dancing. I made sure that I learnt the proper technique of dance and then I used to follow the syllabus. I am happy to say that I received solid traditional Kathak training over many years in India, and I enjoy performing and certainly have a lot of teaching experience.

11   Differences of Indian classical dance between north India and south India

Mrs Nilima Devi explains the differences of Indian classical dance between north and South India thus:

One major difference between north and south Indian classical dance styles apart from their distinct methods of using dance techniques and costumes is that they have different music systems, following the northern and the southern tradition of Indian music respectively. In our *Sinjini* DVD, a useful educational tool which CICD produced and launched in 2007, we are illustrating and explaining these various distinctions and special characteristics of the different dance forms and also present the different musical instruments. In Indian classical dance as a whole there are seven different styles, coming from the north (Kathak), the South (Bharatnatyam, Kathakali and Mohini Attam), the east (Odissi and Manipuri), and the more central parts of India (Kuchipudi). I am from the northwest and my dance style of Kathak is a north Indian dance style. Nowadays I see that north Indian and south Indian dances are taught everywhere in India and also elsewhere, including England.

In traditional training, the teachers are not mixing the different dance styles. A particular tradition is learnt separately, and there are sub-systems or schools (*gharanas* in Kathak style) of the classical dance system. For Kathak dance we have mainly three schools or *gharanas*, from Jaipur (my own), Lucknow and Banaras. Sometimes students learn two or more dance styles and then their movement vocabulary becomes hybrid and of course many combinations are possible. All over England today, it depends very much who happens to be teaching dance in a particular city or place. The picture is very different in the various parts of the country. In Leicester the focus has been on north Indian dance training, basically Kathak is taught here because of me, and now some of my students. In Leicester Bharatnatyam is also taught, but is not as prominent as in London and Birmingham, where there are very good south Indian dance teachers.

12   Differences between Indian classical dance and Bollywood dance[13]

Mrs Nilima Devi explains the differences between Indian classical dance and Bollywood dance.

Indian classical dance takes many years of training as a dancer because it is such a formally structured system of movement and expression. In the case of Bollywood dance, it is much more flexible and improvised and one may be able to learn the steps fairly easily and then can perform such a dance after a short period of training or practice. It depends, sometimes it may take two weeks, sometimes if you are very good, it will take just one week of rehearsals. You just learn for a year, and then you can do lots of Bollywood dancing. However, there are definitely big differences of quality and standard also in Bollywood dancing. In classical dance you have to train systematically and in that respect, too, it is like western ballet. You train for years and years, perfecting your technique, building up your dance vocabulary. It can take ten years of training to become a classical Indian dancer and to reach good professional standards.

If you have had classical dance training and you learn Bollywood dancing, it becomes probably easier, because your body and mind are already trained in movement co-ordination. You know how to move, are aware of how to combine different steps, so you won't fall over, and you are more familiar with the music and different rhythms. If that is the case, then you can learn such forms of dance rather quickly. Bollywood dance has become very popular more recently because people see it all the time in films. It is also quite glamorous, the songs are often really popular and because the film stars are their new heroes, for many young people in particular, they have become like role models, sometimes even like gods. Bollywood has become very popular also in Leicester, confirmed by some recent research. [14] It is very entertaining, but you cannot really compare Bollywood dance and classical dance styles because they also serve very different purposes as art forms. In the past, many of the most prominent Bollywood and film dancers were actually classically trained, and often they were very good indeed. Today's scene of Bollywood dancing is heavily influenced by modern Western and other contemporary styles of dance and movement. The cultural content is often very minimal, and the focus is on rhythm and entertainment. It is all about showmanship and glamour, and of course about money as well.

In the past, they also used to present classical dances in some films, but now it is mostly just Bollywood dance. It is more entertaining and they combine different steps and many quite diffuse dance styles. Sometimes they use folk steps and sometimes classical movements. Sometimes they take modern western dance styles like hip-hop and street dancing, or even incorporate salsa and ballroom dance movements. As all sorts of elements are added into Bollywood dance, it has become a mixture of lots of styles, attractive for entertaining large crowds and big corporate shows, since the main purpose is often show business and thus to make more money. They also add much gymnastics and stunts to these modern dances, so it is sometimes like 'Wow! How did they do that!?' These developments are certainly trying to make dance more popular, and Bollywood dance is today indeed a very prominent form of dance, accessible for all kinds of people. I feel that there is room for all these different dance styles.

Classical dance serves different purposes and is in my view more about education and artistic sophistication than merely hyper-active entertainment. It is based on a set of rules and regulations and there are sophisticated principles in this form of dance, following old books in the ancient Sanskrit language, which few people read and know these days. There is a famous book on dance and drama from the second century AD, the *Abhinayadarpanam* ('Mirror of Gestures').[15] It talks in much detail about the use of the hands in dance, for example. So as classically trained dancers we may follow that guidance, and this then leads to very systematic classical training. This does not mean that innovation is not possible, but first one learns the traditional basics, and then one experiments with new additions. In Bollywood dancing it is not like that.

Classical dance also has its own repertoire of stories, many taken from mythology and ancient texts, such as the major epics Mahabharata and Ramayana. But of course you can also perform contemporary stories through the medium of classical dance. Once you know the classical dance style, you can actually improvise a lot, especially in Kathak dance. One can really perform any story, just becoming different characters all the time, it depends on your skill and imagination. Traditional Kathak was a solo dance, but modern forms of Kathak are increasingly experimenting with group choreography. Once you do that, then of course the form of presentation can be really different in comparison to one single dancer having to be all kinds of characters within minutes.

Traditionally we offer the audience a combination of more rhythm-based 'technical' dance items and then some more expressional pieces, including one or more of the big traditional Indian mythological stories or some smaller pieces of devotional character, like stories about Krishna and Radha. The traditional training syllabus covers all of that, and so we are trained within a kind of school tradition (*gharana* in Kathak) to perform a quite diverse and rich traditional repertoire. A skilful dancer will choose her items for presentation depending on the purpose of the performance and the anticipated audience. We see nowadays that every dancer seems to develop his or her own specific ways of performing and does not necessarily stick to his or her 'school tradition'. In effect, there is a lot of borrowing of ideas and copying of movements and attractive elements. Everybody wants to be 'on show', and we are constantly innovating. To present classical dance as merely 'traditional' and static is therefore a misrepresentation, as a dancer who performs in this day and age is actually also a 'contemporary' dancer. Of course in the wide field of classical dance, if you want to remain a dancer and performer, it is a life-long vocation and you keep on training and learning. One famous Kathak dancer from Pune in India, Guru Pandita Rohini Bhate, who died in 2008 at the age of 84, danced well into her late seventies and taught senior disciples right to the end of her life. She also came to Leicester at some point and delighted us with some memorable performances.

II The Life Story of Mrs Nilima Devi, MBE

13   Leicester as a multi-ethnic city

Leicester reminded Mrs Nilima Devi of the city of Vadodara where she came from in Gujarat. She recalls Leicester and Vadodara thus:

Leicester and different religious establishments

Leicester is a very diverse city and there are many different communities living here in different parts of the town and its surroundings. Generally speaking, the areas closer to the city centre are traditional areas of concentrations of ethnic minorities. But nowadays, mainly due to social mobility, many earlier migrants have moved into more suburban areas and there is much diversity everywhere now. It is not possible to speak of one particular segregated area, though it is still the case that the Belgrave area of Leicester is home to many East African Asians, while the Highfields area of Leicester today is more and more dominated by various kinds of Muslims, now also from Somalia and other parts of the world. The Leicester Central Mosque[16] near the station wasn't built when we first came to the city. In our own neighbourhood, where there has now for many years been a Bengali mosque at the end of our street, it all started to change more visibly when more Bengalis came to live in this area, Muslim Bengalis from Bangladesh who brought over their families and then opened shops and other businesses.

More recently, Somalis have been doing the same, and even more recently, there has been a significant influx of people from Eastern Europe, especially Poland and now from Slovakia. The Evington Road area of the city today has a very different ethnic composition and appearance from a few decades ago. It is today dominated by Panjabi Muslims, many of whom seem to have come from Bradford and other places further north in England. They are coming here because Leicester is thought to be a fairly rich city where they could find jobs and open businesses. More recently, some new Polish and Slovakian shops have come up in our area, too. Earlier there were quite a few Sikhs in that same area, but they seem to have moved to other parts of the city. In some locations of Leicester, you see several big Gurdwaras (Sikh temples) and there are quite a few Hindu temples, and of course many mosques and Muslim places of religious education. As an industrial city in the centre of England, Leicester seems to have always attracted migrants from all over the world. Earlier it was mainly Gujarati Hindus and Panjabi Hindus and Sikhs, many from East Africa. More recently, the existing diversity within Leicester has become even more complex.

I went to Hindu temples many times, sometimes also to perform there and sometimes to teach dance. When my mother used to be here earlier, we sometimes went for a celebration or some function, and we saw this mainly as an occasion to meet people. I would take her to the temple, but not so much for worship as in relation to social functions or connected to my dance activities. I think about Lord Krishna or Lord Shiva when I dance, as I also see dance as a form of meditation. I have some images of gods in my house but just worship at home, not in temples, because there are so many people at

II The Life Story of Mrs Nilima Devi, MBE

these temples, especially if there is a special celebration. Somehow, I never liked big crowds, so I am not a regular visitor to these temples. When I go, it is a short stay. You go there and pray and sometimes you offer flowers and then you take blessed food (*prasad*) and you go. So many people come and go, all the time.

Leicester and Vadodara, Gujarat state

I find Leicester a beautiful city and like it very much. There is a lot happening here and I am very comfortable living in Leicester. I feel that there is still more to do and to contribute to the city of Leicester, although in the past thirty years I have done a lot of work relating to dance. I still feel I need to continue with my dance work until I find the right person to carry on this work, because it is so important for the younger generation to learn about these traditions and their connections to culture and to life in general. I still haven't found anybody who can do that but I remain hopeful that I will find someone one day. I don't think I will ever retire, as I am inspired to still help other, mainly younger people, especially other young artists and dancers, to contribute to the cultural development of the city and to continue work on Indian classical dance forms, especially Kathak. Some of my students have become very good ambassadors for the city of Leicester in the global arts world, and I am very proud of them.

Leicester reminded me of the city of Vadodara in Gujarat, where I come from, when I first came to the UK. It really looked like my home town, with lovely open parks and a good road system. There are lots of Indians living here who speak Gujarati, so it felt like home. It is a beautiful green city and there are lots of shops where you can buy all kinds of Indian food. When I was in Germany it was very difficult to find certain vegetables, but here you can buy everything. It is also easy to travel from one place to another, not like in London. These days, however, Vadodara is much more congested than Leicester, and the city has become really huge, with more than four million inhabitants. Where there used to be huge fields before, this is now a heavily urbanised city environment, with whole new suburbs. Leicester in comparison has remained compact and more peaceful and it is certainly less hectic. When I was young, Vadodara was a very nice peaceful city. Now this is very different and I do feel more at home in Leicester.

14   Asian dance in Leicester in the twenty-first century [17]

Mrs Nilima Devi reflects on more recent developments in her field of expertise and activities and explains her visions for the future thus:

Having worked over several decades in partnership with many others, and based on strong public support over many years especially in the 1980s and 1990s, after about 2002, I see that the Asian dance scene in Leicester has significantly changed. While I am still teaching Kathak in our studio at the Institute, there are now many more people teaching different Indian dance styles. Most notably, Bollywood dancing, as we saw earlier, has become a prominent feature in the city's involvement with Indian dance.

There is a lot going on, but the various efforts and developments remain un-coordinated and thus do not have the impact that one might hope they should have, given the prominence of the Asian population of Leicester in the city's demographic make-up. There is, for example, no major Asian Arts Centre, it is spread all over the city.

New dance developments in and around Leicester since the Millennium have been mainly based on project funding, for which one has to first of all make an application. This can be very laborious and is not really what a trained classical dancer should be doing. This kind of task should be managed and handled by dedicated staff. However, if there is no funding support for administrative staff, then this task falls back on the dancer who wants to see her vision take shape. So I have continued to battle on and spend a lot of time in meetings and on project applications, time that I would much rather spend on artistic work.

Because Leicester and CICD had such a strong earlier track record of Asian dance development, we were successful in obtaining Regional Arts Council Lottery Project (RALP) funding for 2003-5, which allowed CICD to provide further advanced dance training for existing groups, nurturing a new generation of dance tutors and teachers. It also made it possible to arrange a new series of showcase performances, which specifically presented new regional talent. In some remarkable cases, this has helped to propel new national and even international star dancers such as Aakash Odedra – and now also Subhash Viman – to a much higher level of publicity and prominence. Aakash started training with me in Kathak as a very young boy, when my own sons were still quite young. One of his first roles was as Mooghli in a rendition of *The Jungle Book* in 1990. He has certainly come a long way since then! Subhash suddenly appeared on the scene as a young man, strong in body and spirit, and ready to combine Kathak movements with all kinds of street dancing, which he put to excellent effect earlier in training up an amazingly versatile multi-cultural youth dance group called 'Special Batch'. Their performances took Leicester stages by storm for a couple of years. Subhash is now working on his own dance productions and like Aakash combines his knowledge and skills in traditional Indian dance styles with contemporary dance vocabulary.

In Leicester itself, between 2006 and 2009, various community cohesion projects [18] focused on the potential role of dance to bring people from different communities together. In many ways, I think, this can be related back to very early developments in the dance scene of Leicester that I am aware of even though I was not yet in the UK then. During the 1970s, before I came to Leicester, De Montfort Hall put on community dance shows that involved various Asian and Eastern European dance groups [19] to compare notes and enjoy each other's performances. The more recent Community Cohesion projects of the new millennium were less focused on Eastern Europeans, but now sought to involve a range of different Asian communities and also several English school groups. But above all, they also began to include different age groups in presenting dance items. This was a real step forward, quite in the spirit of the funders.

II   The Life Story of Mrs Nilima Devi, MBE

To see young children, for the first time in their life, perform a dance on stage is quite familiar to me as a dance teacher – one often encounters excited parents and grandparents who go through that experience. But when a few minutes later grandmothers, who had never been given a change or had the courage to come forward for dance activities, appeared on stage, this was quite something! We also learnt from this enchanting experience that dance activities relate very closely to health, including mental health. The sheer joy of performing and sharing one's skills with others led to strong realisation that we should now develop more dance projects that portray dance as a health-related activity, and also offer this for older people. In the last few years, this is what has been happening, with absolutely amazing effects.

Side by side with activist engagement in projecting new forms of dance and new groups of participants in dance activities, CICD has also been taking a leading role by organising regional and national conferences on Asian dance development. In 2000, such a conference, held at the Knighton Fields Dance and Drama Centre in Leicester, brought together practitioners and critics from all over the country. Another national conference was held at Leicester University in 2005. Some of the papers from that conference are published.[21] Both venues permitted the combination of theoretical and policy-focused debate with the delightful presentation of new dance work by various groups from all over the country. This kind of cross-regional sharing was continued when on 28 October 2011, at the Curve Theatre in Leicester, we celebrated the 30th birthday of CICD with another National Dance Symposium, 'Moving On'. This was a fairly large conference focusing on succession planning, the future development of Asian dance forms in the UK, and the crazily complex challenges faced by South Asian dancers trying to survive as artists rather than multi-tasking all-rounders.[20]

I feel strongly that the future of South Asian dance in the UK, in fact anywhere in the world, will depend critically on the presence and guidance of solidly trained exponents of the major classical dance styles. If that heritage is lost, the ground will slip from under our feet. As dancers, we may float in the air, but will not be grounded anymore in what it means to present an ancient story, or a simple global truth about right and wrong. If the connections of Indian dance forms with their founding cultural environments are completely broken, the dance that emerges may still be attractive and innovative, but it may be sterile and meaningless. It can still be beautiful art and exciting movement, but it lacks a link to what it means to be Indian or Asian, or to be a classical Indian dancer who knows what her cultural roots are. I am thus concerned that a combination of lack of funding and loss of cultural connectivity will weaken the entire field of classical Indian dance and will lead to its replacement, as we already see in much of the Bollywood presentations, by stereotypical images and snippets of what it means to be South Asian or Indian, projected into diaspora, and thus doubly alienated. While I do believe that solid dance training of young people also in places like England can produce a next generation of what we call 'exponents' of dance traditions, the real experts continue to be raised in India itself. This is why I have found it so important to encourage our most promising students to arrange trips to India, to engage with dance professionals there, and to learn more about the very many roots of the many beautiful Indian dance forms that can still nourish the continuation of traditional dance forms like Kathak.

I am not saying that tradition should simply be preserved and reproduced *per se* and for its own sake. As I outlined earlier, every dancer, when (s)he presents a dance item, gives it a unique stamp and re-creates something that has traditional roots and branches, but is also very much a product of the here and now. This lived presence, also today, and more so in multicultural places such as Leicester, is not just a uniform one-size-fits-all entity, but a very situation-specific and highly sophisticated cultural construct. It constantly develops, it is not dead or static. As an art form, dance entertains and maybe conveys some messages. In both the performer and the audience, according to the ancient Indian *rasa* theory, which concerns a complex theory of sentiments, something is happening when one dances or watches a dance. This may have the effect to transform everyone, as it makes people realise their connectedness to everything else. Dance activities are not just a physical and visible or audible form of movement, then. They are also a form of meditation, as I have said for many years.

Indeed, engaging with dance also moves the mind, as the recent experiences of the aptly named RASIKA[21] dance project in Leicester so clearly confirmed. In that remarkable performance in 2014, mentally impaired and disabled individuals presented themselves on stage and wowed a surprised audience by the sheer beauty of simple yet structured movements. Dance, this confirms, can be therapeutic, both for the performer and the audience. As such it continues to fulfil an important role in the many kinds of human activities that we engage in. As a professional dancer who has dedicated her life to this activity, I can clearly see that till the end of my days I want to be involved in dance. The worry about who will carry on what I have been building up and developing over the years is there. However, I am also confident that others do share this inspirational approach and will thus in future somehow carry on the work that is presently going on.

Notes

1. Vadodara (formerly Baroda) was capital of one of the richest princely states in pre-Independence India. The old town has a number of attractions associated with the ruling maharajas.(Maria Lord (ed.), *Insight Guides India*, London: Discovery Channel [APA Publications], p. 287).
2. For Maharashtra, see *Ibid*, pp.276-281.
3. Sindhis are an ethnic group of people, originating from Sindh, a province of present Pakistan. After the 1947 indepedece of India and Pakistan, many Sindhi Hindus migrated to India and some later to other parts of the world. Some Sindhi Hindus believe in tenets of Sikhism, and can be regarded as concurrently following Hinduism and Sikhism. For the history of Sindhi, see Claude Markovits, *The Global World of Indian Merchants, 1750-1947*, Cambridge: Cambridge University Press, 2000; Matthew A. Cook, Michael Boivin, *Interpreting the Sindhi World: Essays on*

Society and History, Oxford: Oxford University Press, 2010; Nandita Bhavnani, *The Making of Exile: Sindhi Hindus and the Partition of India*, Tranquebar, 2014.

4   Kathak, a dance from North India, uses mime and body techniques to tell stories. Much of Kathak dance is based on intricate rhythmic patterns and musical mathematics (Colin Hyde, Smita Vadnerkar & Angela Cutting (compiled), *Parampara: Thirty years of Indian dance and music in Leicester*, Leicester: A Living History Unit Publication, Leicester City Council, 1996, p.46).

5   On the 4th of August 1972, the then President of Uganda, Idi Amin, announced the expulsion of his country's Asian population. Giving them 90 days to leave, he declared that non-African Ugandans were no longer needed in Uganda. As a result, residents of Asian origin left Uganda for India, Pakistan, Canada, the United States, Australia and Europe. A number of them held British passports, and over 27,000 South Asians migrated to Britain, around 6,000 of them to the city of Leicester. For the Ugandan expulsion in 1972, see Valerie Marett, *Immigrants Settling in the City*, Leicester: Leicester University Press, 1989; do., 'Resettlement of Ugandan Asians in Leicester', *Journal of Refugee Studies*, vol.6, no.3, 1993, pp.248-59.; Z. Lalani (compiled), *Ugandan Asian Expulsion: 90 Days and Beyond Through the Eyes of the International Press*, London: Expulsion Publications, 1997; Kiyotaka Sato (ed.), *Life Story of Mr Jaffer Kapasi, OBE: Muslim Businessman in Leiester, and the Ugandan Expulsion in 1972*, Tokyo: Research Centre for the History of Religious and Cultural Diversity (Meiji University), 2012.

6   For the Hindu wedding ceremony, see Raj Bali Pandey, *Hindu Samskāras (Socio-Religious Study of the Hindu Sacraments)*, Delhi: Motilal Banarsidass, 1969.

7   Highfields, one of the inner-city areas of Leicester, is in the southeast of the city. The area has a large ethnic minority population. It contains Indian, Jewish, Irish, Polish, Somali, Pakistani, African-Caribbean and Eastern European communities. There are also many religious establishments such as a synagogue (this is now closed), various Christian churches, Hindu temples, Sikh temples (gurdwaras) and many mosques (see *Highfields Remembered*, Leicester: Leicestershire County Council/De Montfort University, 1996; Penny Walker (ed.), *We are South Highfields: Life in Our Area, Past & Present*, Great Britain: Near Neighbours, 2012; http://highfields.dmu.ac.uk/text/CO_list.html).

8   Belgrave district lies a mile and a half northeast of the centre of Leicester. The large Asian community based in and around Belgrave Road have been residents since in the early 1970s. See Seliga, Joseph, 'A Neighbourhood Transformed: the Effect of Indian Migration on The Belgrave Area of Leicester, 1965-1995', *The Local Historian*, vol.28, no.4, 1998; pp.225-41; Christine Jordan, *The Illustrated History of Leicester's Suburbs*, Derby: The Breedon Books Publishing, 2003, pp.31-56; Bill Law & Tim Haq (written & edited), with chapters by Professor Richard Bonney & Bernard Greaves, *Belgrave Meomories: 1945 to 2005*, Heritage Lottery Funded, East Midlands Economic Network, 2007; do., *Belgrave Memories: Tales of Belgrave Transcripts, 1945 to 2005, Sixty Years of Heritage*, East Midlands Economic Network, 2007; Michael Smith, *The Story of Belgrave: the Life and Death of a Leicestershire Village*, Birstall: Birstall Local History Society, 2013; Kiyotaka Sato

(ed.), *The Life Story of Mr Ramanbhai Barber, MBE, DL: The President of the Shree Sanatan Mandir in Leicester*, Tokyo: Research Centre for the History of Religious and Cultural Diversity (Meiji University), 2015.

9 For the history of the Centre for Indian Classical Dance (CICD), see Colin Hyde, Smita Vadnerkar & Angela Cutting (compiled), *op.cit.*; Centre for Indian Classical Dance, *Karman: History of South Asian Dance in Leicester and Leicestershire*, Leicester, 2012 (Compiled by Cynthia Brown and Werner Menski).

10 For the Asian Dance Animateur Project, see *Ibid*, pp.40-41.

11 The word Navratri means 'nine nights' in Sanskrit. Hindu festival performed over nine nights, with Garba (a Gujarati clap dance) and Raas (a Gujarati stick dance) dancing in honour of the Goddess Amba. Navratri is an important major festival and is celebrated all over India and in the Indian diaspora. (Hyde, Colin, Vadnerkar, Smita & Cutting, Angela (compiled), *op.cit.*; Kiyotaka Sato (ed.), *Mr Ramanbhai Barber, op.cit.*, Appendix 12 (passim).

12 Diwali is mainly a Hindu festival, although the Sikhs and the Jains celebrate it for different reasons. In Hinduism it is the celebration of the victory of prince Ram over the evil demon-king Ravana. The story shows the triumph of good over evil. It is, therefore, called 'the festival of lights'. In this festival, people light up their houses and shops. Diwali celebrations in Leicester are one of the biggest outside of India, with up to tens of thousands people attending the switching on ceremony of lights on the Belgrave Road and Melton Road, and even more attending Diwali day itself in the heart of the city's Asian community. It started in 1983 in Leicester. It is celebrated twenty days after Navratri (http://www.leicester.gov.uk/your-council-services/lc/events/major-events/diwali2012); Vernon Davis, *Leicester Celebrates: Festivals in Leicester Past & Present*, Leicester: Leicester City Council Living History Unit, 1996, pp.69-71; Kiyotaka Sato (ed.), *Mr Ramanbhai Barber, op.cit.*, Appendix 6 (pp.119-128), Appendix 12 (passim).

13 For Bollywood in Leicester, see Ann R. David, 'Performing Faith: Dance, Identity and Religion in Hindu Communities in Leicester and London', Unpublished PhD thesis (De Montfort University), 2005; do., 'Beyond the Silver Screen: Bollywood and Film Dance in the UK', *South Asia Research*, 27 (1): 5-24.

14 For some recent research, see note 13.

15 Ananda Coomaraswamy, *The Mirror of Gesture*. New Delhi: Munshiram Manoharlal. (An English translation of the ancient text Abhinayadarpanam), 1977.

16 This Sunni mosque, owned by the Islamic Centre, was the second mosque to be established in Leicester. Work began in 1965 to convert a former dance hall at 2A Sutherland Street, a premises purchased by the Pakistan Association. By 1982 a new site was sought and in 1986 the Conduit Street site (1.35 acres) was acquired from Leicester City Council (Richard Bonney, *Understanding and Celebrating Religious Diversity: The Growth of Diversity in Leicester's Places of Religious Worship since 1970*, Leicester: Centre for the History of Religious and Political Pluralism, University of Leicester, 2003, pp.95-97).

17 For the future development of Asian dance forms in the UK, see Naseem Khan, *The Arts Britain Ignores: The Arts of Ethnic Minorities in Britain*. London: Community

Relations Commission, 1976; Centre for Indian Classical Dance, *op.cit.*, pp.65-79.
18 The 'Cantle Report' was produced in December 2001 and made 70 recommendations. The concept of 'community cohesion' was subsequently adopted by the Labour government and Ted Cantle was asked to chair the panel which advised ministers on implementation. Community cohesion refers to the aspect of togetherness and bonding exhibited by members of a community, the 'glue' that holds a community together. The Institute of Community Cohesion is a not-for-profit organisation established in 2005 to provide a new approach to diversity and multiculturalism. Its work focuses on building positive and harmonious community relations, using applied research to develop practice constantly, and to build capacity locally, nationally and internationally to promote community cohesion. (http://www.idea.gov.uk/idk/core/page.do?paged=1600021; www.communities.gov.uk/documents/…/buildingcohesivecommunities.pdf; Ted Cantle, *Community Cohesion: A Report of the Independent Review Team*, Home Office, 2001; Ted Cantle, *Community Cohesion: A New Framework for Race and Diversity*, Basingstoke: Palgrave Macmillan, 2005; Margaret Wetherell, Michellynn Lafleche & Robert Berkeley (eds), *Identity, Ethnic Diversity and Community Cohesion*, London: SAGA, 2007; John Flint & David Robinson, *Community Cohesion in Crisis?: New Dimensions of Diversity and Difference*, Bristol: The Policy Press, 2008; *Community Cohesion and Migration: Tenth Reports of Session 2007-8*, by authority of the House of Commons, London: The Stationary Office Limited, 2008.
19 For East European dance groups, Kiyotaka Sato (ed.), *The Life Story of Mr Andrejs Ozolins, a Latvian, and His Wife Mrs Dulcie Ozolins*, Tokyo: Research Centre for the History of Religious and Cultural Diversity (Meiji University), 2014, passim.
20 See Ann R. David, (2007), *op.cit.*; Andrée Grau, 'Political Activism and South Asian Dance: The Case of Mallika Sarabhai', *South Asia Research*, 27(1), 2007, pp. 43-55; Stacey Prickett, '*Guru* or Teacher? *Shishya* or Student? Pedagogic Shifts in South Asian Dance Training in India and Britain', *South Asia Research*, 27(1), 2007, pp. 25-41.
21 The term is a modification of the term 'Rasa', basically meaning mood or feeling, and in this case, was created as a term for this context by Nilima, here it means 'a female who is interested in health and well-being'.

III
Addendum to the book on Nilimaji

III Addendum to the book on Nilimaji

My perspectives on why we are, and remain, in Leicester: Werner Menski

This work is about my wife, Nilima Devi and her contributions as a Kathak dance artist to the multicultural environment of our beautiful home city, Leicester. But clearly, without my involvement we would not be here, and Nilimaji would not have achieved what she has been able to do. I thus agree with Professor Sato that I should maybe add another layer of diversity to the accounts presented here, also given that our marriage and the unique way in which our family was brought about and came to Leicester is part of this book. Also, I remain actively involved in Asian dance development in Leicester as Chair of the Board of Directors of CICD, the Centre for Indian Classical Dance that Nilima Devi has been running for over thirty years, and should say a bit more about that.

My own background is originally as far removed from classical Indian dance as one can imagine. I grew up on a large farm in Northern Germany, which from early childhood onwards meant being connected to the earth, to nature, and to local and cultural influences on people's lives. As a global citizen, yet rooted in the place I presently live in, I have my feet on the ground, even though we move about a lot. Born in 1949, I was the product of a mixed marriage, though both my parents were German. In the immediate aftermath of World War II a liaison between a local farmer's daughter and an uprooted refugee from faraway Ostpreussen (Eastern Prussia), since 1945 part of Poland, was not an easily acceptable social fact. I actually had a Polish grandmother whom I never met, as she perished on the trek westwards in 1945, during the family's exodus from Eastern Prussia.

Early life in Germany revolved around the farm and its never-ending work routines. After initial struggles, since I did not know any German until the age of five and spoke only the local dialect, Plattdeutsch, an ancestor language of English, I actually enjoyed going to school and learning things. Apparently, the brilliant primary schoolmaster (who I later learnt was also from Ostpreussen and had first met my father in a teacher training college when they were 17 years old) recognised my

Harvesting hay in North Germany, 1954.

potential. He spoke to my father and encouraged him to send me to grammar school. I guess I was anyway not destined to become a farmer, since only one son inherits the land in our tradition, and my younger brother was very early on chosen for that. So I went to grammar school in 1960 in the nearest town, Itzehoe, and began to study Latin there as my first foreign language. A year and a half later though, we had to move to a different farm some sixty kilometres away, and unfortunately (or maybe fortunately) this new school did not offer a choice between English and Latin, but only started with

English. So at the age of 12, I had to speedily learn English within weeks rather than months or years, to be able to catch up with my age group in school. That challenging experience left a lasting impression, as I realised now that I could handle intensive language training. This was useful later when I took French, resumed Latin, tried my hand at Ancient Greek, too, and then a decade later encountered Indian languages. Being at school was quite exciting, as I also began to learn about editing a student journal and gave private tuitions to juniors. This provided some pocket money but also growing awareness and confidence that I was maybe suitable as a teacher. Some excellent role models of highly competent teachers provided further inspiration. I took the German equivalent of 'A' levels (Abitur) in summer 1968 before joining the German army a week later for two years. At that time army service was compulsory. Looking back, that period, too, gave me valuable teaching and mentoring experience, for as a young officer I was soon in charge of the welfare of quite a few young people.

This photo is taken with Ugandan refugee children in Lincolnshire in autumn 1972.

I started studying Geography and English at Kiel University in 1970, still with the aim to become a school teacher. After four semesters, in 1972, the decision to further test my appetite for teaching was to completely change my life and also connected me for the first time to Leicester. In summer 1972, Britain was not yet part of the European Union, so I required a work permit for a position as an Assistant Teacher of German at the City of Leicester School in Downing Drive and Alderman Newton's Boys School near the Cathedral. I had never been to the UK before and had applied for a job specifying that I wanted to be outside London. More or less by chance I was allocated to Leicester. I arrived there, a complete stranger to the UK, via the car ferry from Hamburg to Harwich in August 1972 in my VW car, finding Leicester completely inundated with Ugandan Asians (Marett, 1989). Almost instantly, my own family's partial refugee experience provided a strong link to those partly traumatised newcomers who had to rebuild their lives. I remember meeting a Mr. Chauhan, who had been a tailor in Uganda, sitting in the front room of a house in Highfields, with a sewing machine and a small bundle of cotton cloth with a colourful East African design. He implored me to order a bush shirt, so he could rebuild his business. I wore that shirt for many years and later encountered this enterprising man as a successful shopkeeper on Evington Road.

I partly enjoyed teaching, specifically the 'A' level students. Soon I became so involved with Asians in Leicester that it became necessary to learn Gujarati and to immerse myself further in Asian culture. A young accountancy student from Mombasa, a Gujarati

III Addendum to the book on Nilimaji

Muslim, offered to teach me his language. I still remember how we struggled with the fine intricacies of the Indian alphabet systems with their soft and hard sounds in aspirated and unaspirated form. What a nuisance if one does not understand the basics, which took us both quite a while to grasp. I was not aware then of any books on the subject, all we had was a little pocket book with the basics. But I learnt to speak, at least a bit, and the interest had been created. When I returned to Germany in summer 1973, the decision was quickly made to study more about UK Asians and the Indian subcontinent with its many languages and cultures. My queries about studying Gujarati caused some amusement, but my university did have an Indology department, covering the vast field of South Asian Studies in the same block in which I had been studying English. I had not even noticed this earlier. So now I added the study of Hindi and Sanskrit to my two existing subjects, enrolling for an MA degree, rather than aiming for a German state exam for school teachers. Meanwhile, since teaching rowdy 14 year olds the basics of a foreign language had put me off secondary school teaching, I began to contemplate a university career. I was extremely lucky to be taught Hindi and a lot about Jaina culture by an excellent old Indian professor from Bombay, Prof. Jagdish Chandra Jain, actually a companion of Mahatma Gandhi. Years later, I wrote about that life-changing experience (Menski, 1993) and in 1973 I also met his wife, who fed me lovely Indian food, and his large family, with whom we are keeping close relations even now. I was also fortunate that the German professor of Sanskrit who taught me at Kiel soon needed a research assistant. Doors began to open for a university career, but I had no clue that this would in due course take me back to the UK.

Before that, though, my MA dissertation had to be written. Seeking to combine the three academic areas of Social Geography, English and Indian or South Asian Studies, in 1976/77 I selected a pioneering field research project focused on Asian retail trade in Leicester. Nobody had ever done anything like this; indeed some people murmured something about madness. Yet I had seen first-hand earlier how Ugandan Asian refugees rebuilt their lives and knew of many Asian shops in various parts of the city, but significantly – then – there were none in Leicester's city centre. So I mapped the entire city area to analyse how Asian businessmen had been resettling in this urban environment, basically reconstructing their own city centre, today's 'Golden Mile' on Belgrave Road. Returning to Leicester many times after 1973, I could not believe what I saw one day: A Gujarati man from Canada walked into a jewellers shop on Belgrave Road with a lump of gold, asking the owner to produce beautiful jewellery for his daughter's wedding! There were many Asian shops along Belgrave Road, some of them still there today. Many more, I knew, were spread all over Highfields and around Narborough Road, but I discovered quite a few more also in far-flung corners, some in (then) completely 'white' areas. My MA thesis, written in German and unpublished (Menski, 1977), proved the hypothesis that Asians were engaged in constructing an alternative city centre in Leicester. I also found that many Asian shops were not just local convenience stores, or operated in some kind of narrow Asian niche, but they attracted customers from all over the UK, Sweden, Canada and many other places. So this was actually an emerging international ethnically-defined business centre! I also noticed during interviews that Asians from London visiting relatives and friends in Leicester filled their car boots, mostly in shops along Narborough Road, before taking the motorway back to the pricier capital. More than 20 years later, our older son did a follow-up geographical study of some of the same shops and found that the earlier patterns were still visible (Menski, 2001). Meanwhile, though, Asian shops had begun to penetrate the traditional city centre as well, but the Golden Mile of Belgrave Road was now an international tourist attraction.

In 1975, on one of my repeat visits to Leicester, an Asian friend suggested that I should buy a house in Leicester. This turned out to be the former Polish butcher's shop in Churchill Street, then owned by a Gujarati Patel family who did not quite dare open a business and wanted to move to a better residential area. So now I had my own home in Leicester, which became quite crucial five years later, when we had a young family, but certainly not enough money to settle in London where I had secured a university job. In between Nilima Devi entered into my life in 1979, and in this book she tells her own story of how she first arrived in Germany and then we decided to settle in Leicester. We both clearly found much that attracted us to the city, and so we are still here!

This photo depicts building the first dance studio at the back of 50 Churchill Street, in September 1980.

Nilima has also told the story of our marriage, and I do not have much to add, except saying perhaps that I admire her for her courage and sustained determination, without which this life project of the Centre for Indian Classical Dance would not have matured. While our two sons grew up and soon developed into highly skilled cultural navigators, we two beavered away at making sure the bills were paid and the people of Leicester were learning more about Indian dance.

A family trip in Leicestershire, 1988.

I observed how our boys had to find their own way through the multiple challenges of being at a large, very diverse secondary school in Leicester during the 1990s, but we kept them busy and focused and we engaged them at home in various ways. Having been warned that as mixed kids they would have no community to fall back on, they both became strong and self-reliant in this multicultural environment, while establishing lasting friendships across all kinds of imagined cultural divides. A lot of Leicester people from all walks of life have moved on, including our sons. An African schoolmate of our younger one, who already as a young boy

III   Addendum to the book on Nilimaji

Multicultural Christmas in Leicester, 1996.

wanted to become a pilot, is now flying Virgin Atlantic planes around the world. The schools that these young people went to may not have offered the smoothest experience of education, but they provided solid groundings to focused students who had a secure home life. And the experience of growing up in a deeply multi-cultural environment certainly makes you more aware of who you are and maybe also how one may handle all sorts of crises and problems that are bound to crop up in such highly diverse and intensely competitive scenarios. In retrospect, the decision to focus on solid English language skills as a foundation for the education of our children in such an environment, but then also from a certain age building on that by cultivating knowledge of several other languages, has proved one of the keys to success in this highly competitive global world. The price one pays is then that a place like Leicester can no longer be home, even though it is a large city, as it simply does not offer the kind of high-level chances that are available in the major global business centres. So we are an extremely international family not only by descent, upbringing and background, but also in terms of our geographical spread today.

Since as a family we were always so focused on dance development in Leicester, I have of course many recollections of what it was like to establish and help run an Indian dance school in the middle of England. Gradually, the hustle and bustle of the dance classes in our studio spilt over into the home. Many of the dance students and their families have become friends over time, and the next generation of young dancers is now appearing, as former students are starting to bring their daughters to CICD to learn Kathak dance. From days past, I remember most vividly coming home from London late one night and the whole lounge was full of our senior Kathak students, busy sewing and preparing the brilliant flowing white dresses that they were going to wear as the swans in the final dance of *The Ugly Duckling* (see p.76, picture 26). The many tours we did all over the country are too numerous to recount, and more often than not I was the driver of the bus or car that took our young artists safely back home. One night I was so tired on the way back from southern England that I missed exit 21 on the M1 motorway and simply drove straight on! One may call that social service, or some kind of labour of love, but it all contributed to the constant excitement of putting together new shows and yet more innovative projects for presentation in showcase performances. We were technically not a family business, but I think in many ways we were. And since I continue to act as the Chair of the Board of Directors of CICD in Leicester, I remain quite closely involved in monitoring new developments and helping to steer the often quite dramatic journey of Kathak dance in Leicester, the wider region, and in the UK.

We celebrated Nilima's achievements of 30 years of CICD in 2011 and the award of her

MBE in 2013 with considerable pride and gratitude to many people in Leicester who had provided us with many kinds of support. I am now officially retired and enjoy my new position of Emeritus Professor. I am trying to slow down but still produce quite a few publications and continue to mentor young people. I remain fascinated by the ongoing constant process of socio-cultural changes and new developments in multicultural Leicester, reputedly one of the most diverse cities in Europe. I may as yet get more involved in researching some topics related to that more directly again, but focus at the moment on writing books about Indian law and Hindu law, in particular. Nilima, so much is sure and is also confirmed through what she tells us in this book, is in no way ready yet to give up her intense involvement in South Asian dance development. I think this is good for her and for us, and it will also be good for Leicester. But there is growing awareness that younger people have to come to the fore now to take on more responsibilities and to carry on what has been developed over so many years. Otherwise the history of Indian dance in Leicester will become a subject matter of archives or files in cupboards and filing cabinets, rather than an ongoing vibrant, living history, which it fortunately still is now. I hope we will have many more years of active involvement for the benefit of all the people of this wonderful city, our hometown, our very own *desh pardesh* (home abroad), as one of my friends, the Manchester-based social anthropologist Roger Ballard, has called this.

References

Ballard, Roger (ed.) (2006 [1994]) *Desh Pardesh: The South Asian Presence in Britain*. London: Hurst & Company.
Marett, Valerie (1989) *Immigrants Settling in the City: Ugandan Asians in Leicester*. Leicester: Leicester University Press.
Menski, Martin (2001) *Reconceptualising the Geography of the Asian Niche Market: A Critical Analysis of the Viability of Asian Retail Businesses in the UK*. London: SOAS (unpublished Geography ISP Dissertation).
Menski, Werner (1977) *Verteilungs-und Funktionsmerkmale des asiatischen Einzelhandels in englischen Industriestädten, dargestellt am Beispiel von Leicester*. (Distributional and Functional Patterns of Asian Retail Trade in English Industrial Cities, illustrated through the Example of Leicester). Kiel: University of Kiel. (Unpublished MA thesis).
Menski, Werner (1980) 'Einwanderer in Großbritannien'. In: *anglistik und englischunterricht* 10 [1980], pp. 125-138.
Menski, Werner (1993) 'From alu ke paraunthe to Jain law'. In Bhattacharya, N. N. (ed.): *Jainism and Prakrit in Ancient and Medieval India. Essays for Prof. Jagdish Chandra Jain*. New Delhi: Manohar, pp. 23-30.

IV
Appendices

IV   Appendices

Appendix 1: Nilima Devi in India and wedding

Nilima being awarded a trophy for her dance performance at the Maharaja Sayajirao University (M.S. University) of Baroda (later Vadodara), 1971.

Nilima performing the Peacock Dance at M.S. University of Baroda, Gujarat, India, 1972.

Nilima tying dancing bells for a performance at the M.S. University of Baroda, 1972.

Nilima offering flowers to Lord Shiva, the Supreme Dancer, at the beginning of her performance, Baroda 1972.

Nilima waiving a lamp for Lord Shiva at the M.S. University of Baroda, 1972.

IV   Appendices

Nilima's friend, Neelam Sule, singing with an orchestra at a Baroda community hall, 1972.

Nilima singing with an orchestra at a Baroda community hall, 1972.

Nilima dancing to poetry at the M.S. University of Baroda, 1973.

Nilima in a Kathak pose at the Baroda Music College, 1973.

Nilima expressing emotion through dance, Baroda, 1973.

IV Appendices

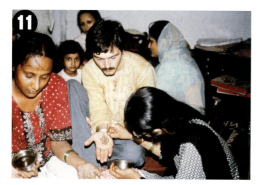

Putting Mehndi (Henna) on Nilima's and Werner's hands on the day before the wedding day, 8 May 1979.

Mehndi (Henna) applied to Nilima's hands and feet in preparation for the wedding rituals, 8 May 1979.

Ritual preparations of the groom by the Hindu priest in Baroda, 9 May 1979.

On the morning of the wedding day, both parties are ritually cleansed by the Haldi (purification) ceremony, in which seven married women touch the cheeks and feet of bride and groom, after which of course there is a need for a bath. In this picture the youngest sister of Nilima's mother applies Haldi to Werner's cheeks.

The groom prays to various Hindu deities to bless the wedding.

IV   Appendices

The bride prays to various Hindu deities to bless the wedding.

Nilima's mother blesses her daughter before the wedding starts, with her younger sister Bhavana looking on.

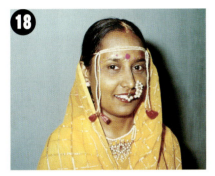

Nilima as a typical Maharashtrian bride before the wedding, 9 May 1979.

Bringing the bride into the wedding hall. In Nilima's family tradition, it is customary that two maternal uncles accompany the bride, carrying swords at the top of which is a lemon. Her sister and a younger cousin are also in this picture.

When the bride has been brought into the wedding hall, she is led behind a large cloth so that the groom cannot yet see her. Then the couple are made to hold hands for the first time (a ritual called *hastagrahana*), while the family and guests sing auspicious songs (*mangalashtaka*) and shower them with flower petals and rice grains. This picture is taken from Nilima's side of the curtain.

IV   Appendices

Still during the hand holding ceremony, this is a picture taken from Werner's side of the curtain, with the maternal uncles and their sword, and the two young ladies behind him.

The next ritual step is the mutual garlanding of bride and groom. In this picture, Nilima is about to garland Werner, with the two maternal uncles now on either side of the parties and everyone looking on.

Werner garlanding Nilima, with everyone looking on.

The garlanded bride and groom, now ready for the next ritual steps.

As part of the wedding rituals, the priest prepares a long string, a sacred thread, with the help of several auspicious, married ladies while bride and groom are seated and wait to be connected with this string.

The couple sit down after having been connected with the sacred string that was prepared earlier.

IV Appendices

Werner ties the wedding necklace (*mangalsutra*) around Nilima's neck while the ladies of the family look on.

Having performed a number of further wedding rituals, especially the walking round the sacred fire (*agniparinayana*) and the ritual of the seven steps (*saptapadi*), Werner and Nilima are now husband and wife according to Hindu law.

The happy spouses now feed each other sweets at the conclusion of the Hindu wedding rituals.

Werner feeding Nilima sweets after the conclusion of the rituals.

Starting from the left, her school friend Rekha, the singer Neelam Sule, her college friend and neighbour Parveen, her sister Bhavana, a Kathak student and a family friend's wife are in the picture.

IV   Appendices

The newly married couple engages in a final prayer to the family deities (*kula devata*) of Nilima's family.

Werner at the start of the evening wedding reception in Baroda, 9 May 1979.

Nilima at the start of the evening wedding reception in Baroda, 9 May 1979.

The couple at the start of their wedding reception in Baroda, 9 May 1979.

Same as fig. 35.

Feeding each other sweets on stage in the evening reception.

IV   Appendices

Werner and Nilima with Nilima's parents in the evening reception.

The couple at the evening reception.

Werner and Nilima with wedding guests.

Werner and Nilima with Nilima's parents and her brother and sister.

Werner and Nilima and the whole maternal family of Nilima.

IV   Appendices

Werner and Nilima with maternal uncles and their families in the evening reception in Baroda.

The couple towards the end of their wedding reception in Baroda, 9 May 1979.

Nilima after a dance performance in Baroda with the organising team, c. 1986.

Nilima with the accompanying musicians after her dance performance in Baroda, 1986.

Nilima with friends and dance students after her performance in Baroda, 1986.

IV Appendices

Appendix 2: Coming to Germany, settling in England, and family visits

Nilima beginning the dance performance during her wedding reception in Germany, 1979.

Nilima telling the story of Radha and Krishna in the same performance in Bochum in 1979.

Nilima telling the story of Rama and Sita living in exile in the forest, Bochum 1979.

Sita trying to catch the deer in that same story, Bochum 1979.

Nilima presenting the story of Krishna and the big snake Kalya, Bochum 1979.

Nilima presenting Krishna dancing on the head of the snake, Bochum 1979.

IV Appendices

Showing emotion through dance, Germany, 1980.

Nilima performing a technical dance piece, Germany, 1980.

Jatayu, the giant bird, flying high to rescue Sita who has been abducted by the wicked Ravana, Germany, 1980.

Ravan cutting the wings of Jatayu, Germany, 1980.

Nilima depicting Jatayu dying, Germany, 1980.

IV   Appendices

Nilima with a group of female relatives and neighbours in Baroda, 1991.

Family visit to Baroda in 1996, Nilima with Martin and Hans and a maternal uncle.

Nilima's maternal cousins in a blessing ritual for Nilima's father, Baroda, 1996.

Nilima with her family in Baroda, c. 1997.

Nilima and son Hans, in Mumbai with her friend, singer Neelam Sule and son Rohan.

Nilima and Werner with family friends in Mumbai.

IV   Appendices

Appendix 3:   Teaching Indian classical dance in Leicester

48-50 Churchill Street in Leicester.(nos. 1-2: photos by the editor, 2013).

The entrance to the Centre for Indian Classical Dance (CICD) in Leicester.

Picture from the opening ceremony of the refurbished CICD studio in Leicester in 1984.

IV   Appendices

Kathak performance at De Montfort Hall, 1986.

Indian folk dance group at De Montfort Hall, 1986.

A Gujarati folk dance called Supra Nritya, 1986.

A Kathak dance demonstration by junior students.

A Kathak workshop in a school, 1986.

A Kathak dance troupe after performing *Kaliya Daman* (see p.154) dance in the park.

IV   Appendices

Scene from *An Evening of Indian Dance*, Leicester 1987.

Kathak dance students in performance for Mahashivaratri, Leicester,

A Gujarati folk dance group at De Montfort Hall, Leicester, 1987.

The Dandiya Raas (stick dance) of Gujarat, 1987.

Dandiya Raas folk dance performance on a stage in the park, 1987.

A Dandiya Raas performance in Houghton-on-the Hill, 1987.

IV   Appendices

The performance of *The Ugly Duckling*. A group of piglets in the farmyard.

Two colourful birds dancing in the farmyard scene.

The cat and the chicken in the farmyard scene.

Two peacocks dancing in the farmyard scene.

The entire group of farmyard animals.

IV Appendices

The performance of *The Ugly Duckling* in 1989. Two newly hatched ducklings.

One of the young ducklings, Leicester 1989.

Another one of the newly hatched ducklings, Leicester 1989.

The Ugly Duckling trying to communicate with the group of ducks on the lake.

Solo dance of Nimisha Patel as the lonely Ugly Duckling, 1989.

Swan dance finale of *The Ugly Duckling*, 1989.

IV   Appendices

Young dancers performing a stick dance at the Haymarket Theatre, Leicester 1989.

A folk dance performance in progress, Leicester.

Pandit Durgalal, one of the great masters of Kathak dance, teaching a master class in Kathak at Arts in Education, 1989.

A Kathak performance with Pandit Durgalal and a team of CICD dancers, Leicester, 1989.

Martin Menski showing Lord Vishnu through Kathak, 1991.

Young musicians on sitar and tabla at a community centre in Leicester, 1991.

77

IV Appendices

The first ever boys' Kathak group performing at a community centre in Leicester, 1991.

The performance of *Seasons of India*, Leicester, 1991.

A group of senior folk dancers on stage, 1991.

Four young dancers at the Jaina Community Centre in Leicester 1991.

Performance of *Seasons of India*, Leicester 1991.

IV   Appendices

Nilima Devi teaching Kathak to her students at Arts in Education, 1992.

Nilima Devi as an engaged Kathak teacher, Arts in Education, 1992.

A contemporary dance workshop by a contemporary dance artist.

A traditional Kathak workshop.

A workshop in the South Indian Bharatnatyam style.

IV Appendices

A story telling workshop.

A special Kathak class for the senior students of Nilima Devi.

Preparations for the performance of *The Arabian Nights* at the Haymarket Theatre, 15 & 16 June 1993.

Nilima and some of the excited participants.

The whole dance team in happy mood after the performance.

A dance workshop for teachers, 'Training the Trainers', with Anusha Subramanyam at the Belgrave Neighbourhood Centre in 1993.

IV   Appendices

Dance workshop for senior students with Kumudini Lakhia from Ahmedabad.

Kathak Dance Workshop for senior students with Kumudini Lakhia.

Two of Nilima's most advanced students performing a Kathak repertoire, Leicester, 1994.

Same as fig. 51.

Students in a Junior School assembly hall, c. 1995.

Nilima demonstrating Kathak poses to a whole school class, c.1995.

IV Appendices

Students of Nilima from Arts in Education performing Tarana, a Kathak technical piece, Leicester, 1996.

Performing a piece of Kathak dance, Leicester, 1996.

Kathak performance at the Haymarket Theatre in Leicester, 1996.

Nilima's students performing Kathak in Leicester, 1996. In front is Aakash Odedra, today a global dance star.

Kathak rhythmic performance (Tarana) at the Haymarket Theatre in 1996.

IV Appendices

Kathak dance performance at Phoenix Theatre in Leicester, 1996.

Kathak dance performance: the whole team of dancers, 1996.

Hans Menski in a Kathak dance performance, 1996.

A young Kathak dancer performing at the Haymarket Shopping Centre, 1998.

A young Kathak dancer, Haymarket Shopping Centre, 1998.

IV Appendices

Nilima and her Leicester and Nottingham Kathak Dance Group.

Nilima giving a presentation on dance in a Hindu temple, Leicester.

Nilima performing a Kathak pirouette in a school's dance demonstration, with Bhupesh Gangani and Munna Lal on tabla and harmonium, 1999.

Nilima and musicians teaching dance in a Leicestershire school, 2001.

IV   Appendices

Nilima teaching the whole class, 2001.

A guest dancer leading an Odissi dance workshop with CICD students, 2002.

An Odissi dance performance for the CICD students.

An Odissi dancer demonstrating specific movement techniques to the class.

IV   Appendices

❼❸

Two samples of thank you notes from schools in which Nilima performed and taught dance. The second note is from the students of Foxton School, the village that has the famous Foxton Locks on the canal system.

IV Appendices

Group photo of the dance and music students of Sangeet Sabha at the Knighton Fields Dance and Drama Centre, Leicester, 2001.

Same as fig. 74.

IV Appendices

Gujarati folk dance, Dandiya Raas, 2003.

Gujarati folk dance, Garba, 2003.

Same as fig. 76.

Same as fig. 76.

Same as fig. 76.

IV   Appendices

Nilima introducing a dance performance in Osaka, 2003.

Nilima with senior students, Nayana Whittaker, Dr. Shashi Mehta, Joy Foxley and Catherine Lowe at the launch of the Sinjini DVD in 2001.

Nilima teaching a school group in Kobe about Indian dance, 2003.

Nilima teaching Indian dance to a whole school class in Kobe, 2003.

IV   Appendices

Nilima performing at a Leicestershire school assembly in 2005.

Nilima teaching Kathak dance to schoolchildren in 2006.

Nilima teaching basic dance moves to children in 2006.

IV   Appendices

Appendix 4: Performance and dance activities of Nilima Devi

Nilima in a Kathak dance pose, 1987.

Same as fig. 1.

Nilima performing with two senior students at the Haymarket Theatre, 1987.

Nilima and a senior student, Gita Lakhlani, performing at the Haymarket Theatre in 1987.

IV Appendices

Nilima performing Kathak at the School of Oriental and African Studies (SOAS), University of London, 1988.

Nilima performing Kathak together with Ghulam Sarwar Sabri on tabla and Nicholas Magriel on sarangi, London 1988.

Nilima the musicians and organisers after the SOAS performance, 1988.

IV   Appendices

Pandit Durgalal and Nilima in a break during their rehearsals, Leicester 1989.

Tabla player Fatehsingh Gangani and dancer Renu Bassi, Leicester, 1989.

Pandit Durgalal and Ashit Desai, the well-known Gujarati singer, 1989.

Pandit Durgalal and Nilima's husband, Leicester 1989.

Group photo of the participants of the Master Class workshop with Pandit Durgalalji, Leicester, August 1989.

IV Appendices

Nilima after a performance in a school in Leicester, c. 1990.

Nilima performing Kathak at the Haymarket Theatre in Leicester, 1990.

Nilima in a Kathak pose at Moat Community College in Leicester, 1991.

Participants in a choreography workshop on the theme of 'Chair' with Kumudini Lakhia, Leicester.

Participants in the 'Chair' dance workshop.

Participants in the workshop, Leicester.

IV   Appendices

Performance of Ganeshstuti by Nilima, Gita Lakhlani and Nayana Whittaker, 1991.

The High Commissioner of India, Dr. L. M. Singhvi, giving a bouquet of flowers to Nilima Devi, Leicester, November 1991.

Nilima introducing a dance item in Derby, with Nilima's dance teacher, Pandit Sunderlal Gangani, on harmonium and Ghulam Sarwar Sabri on tabla, Derby 1991.

Nilima presenting a dance item at Manor House Neighbourhood Centre in Leicester, 1991.

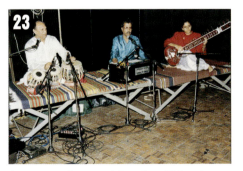

Accompanying musicians in a *Triangle* performance by Nilima Devi. On the left is Nilima's dance teacher, Pandit Sunderlal Gangani (1929-2013), on harmonium Sheetal Mukherjee, with Rupa Panesar on Sitar.

IV   Appendices

Nilima performing Kathak, Leicester, c. 1993.

Nilima in a dance pose taken at the Kadamb Institute in Ahmedabad, 1993.

Same as fig. 25.

IV   Appendices

Nilima performing Kathak in North England, telling a story, 1994.

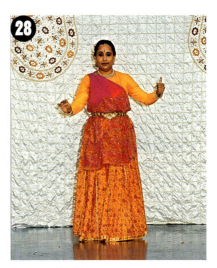

Same as fig.27.

Nilima performing with Gita Upadhya and Priya Pawar at the Guildhall in Leicester, 1994.

The orchestra and dancers for the Guildhall performance in 1994.

IV   Appendices

Nilima performing *Melory* (melody and rhythm) at the Chisenhale Dance Space in London, 1995.

A still from the *Melory* dance performance, 1995.

Nilima performing *Melory* at the Chisenhale Dance Space in London, 1995.

A ballet performance of *La Fille Mal Gardeé* by students of Leicestershire Arts at the Haymarket Theatre, 1995.

Nilima with dancers from the Annapurna Dance Company in Halifax, 1995.

Nilima with Shanta Rao, Director of the Annapurna Dance Company, and young dancer Shane Shambhu, Halifax, 1995.

IV   Appendices

Nilima performing Kathak contemporary piece, *Against the Tide* at the Leicestershire Arts in Education Theatre, 1995

A still from the *Brahmari* performance, 1995

Same as fig.38.

Same as fig. 38.

IV Appendices

Nilima Devi performing a Kathak contemporary piece, *Against the Tide*, at the Leicestershire Arts in Education Theatre, 1995.

Same as fig. 41.

Same as fig. 41.

Same as fig. 41.

IV Appendices

A scene from the ballet performance of *La Fille Mal Gardeé*, 1995.

Same as fig. 45.

Same as fig. 45.

Nilima Devi with Kathak dancers Padma Sharma and her daughter Gauri Sharma at CICD, 1997.

IV   Appendices

Nilima and famous Kathak dancer Damayanti Joshi, Bombay, 1996.

Kathak performance by Nilima in the Kamani Auditorium, Delhi, 1996: Lighting the lamp at the start of the performance.

Nilima receiving flowers from Richa Gupta after the performance, 1996.

Nilima receiving a shawl, with famous Indian Kathak dancer Rajendra Gangani looking on.

IV   Appendices

Nilima performing at the Kamani Auditorium in Delhi, 1996.

Nilima showing the pose of Shiva in Kathak dance, Delhi, 1996.

Guru Pandita Rohini Bhate in an abhinaya (expressions) performance in Leicester, 1997.

Kathak dancer Rochan Datye from Pune demonstrating abhinaya in Leicester, 1999.

IV Appendices

Welcoming of Nilima at the start of her Kathak performance at the South Bank Centre in London, 1998.

Nilima performing a Kathak story at the South Bank Centre in London, 1998.

Same as fig. 58.

IV   Appendices

Nilima leading a dance workshop at the South Bank Centre in London, 1998.

Students participating in the workshop at the South Bank Centre, London, 1998.

Same as fig. 61.

Same as fig. 61.

Nilima showing dance movements with a tabla player, Ghulam Sarwar Sabri, London, 1998.

IV   Appendices

Nilima rehearsing with Priya Pawar and musicians in Baroda, 1998.

Entrance to the Centre for Performing Arts, University of Pune, India.

Kathak Guru Pandita Rohini Bhate (1924-2008) in Pune and her husband, 1999.

A Kathak dance training session with advanced disciples of Rohini Bhate, Pune, 1999.

Rajendra Gangani, one of India's leading Kathak dance exponents, in a lecture demonstration in Pune, 1999.

Nilima with Guru Pandita Rohini Bhate in Pune, 1999.

IV   Appendices

The keynote speaker, Reginald Massey, at the Kathak Conference in Leicester in 2000. Next to him are Werner Menski and Nilima.

Keynote speaker Reginald Massey.

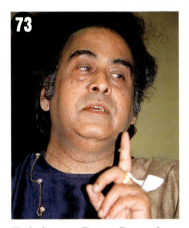

Kathak guru Pratap Pawar from London, at the Leicester Conference in 2000.

Nilima speaking at the Kathak Conference in Leicester, 2000.

David Henshaw, Contemporary Dance Critic, at the Leicester Conference, 2000.

IV Appendices

Kathak dancer Sushma Mehta speaking at the Leicester Conference in 2000.

Kathak dancers Padma Sharma and Pratap Pawar engaged in discussion during the Dance Conference in 2000.

Senior CICD Kathak students in a showcase performance at the Dance Conference in Leicester in 2000.

Quincy Charles, a Kathak dancer originally from Trinidad, performing during the Dance Conference in Leicester in 2000.

IV   Appendices

School workshop participants, Leicestershire, 2000.

Nilima teaching a group of school children, Leicestershire, 2000.

Nilima teaching a workshop at a Leicestershire school, 2000.

A dance workshop in progress, organised by the Imperial Society of Teachers of Dancing (ISTD) at its Congress in Scotland, 2001. ISTD is one of the world's leading dance examination boards.

IV Appendices

Performance of *Vyom (The Dance of the Nine Planets)* by CICD students and dance students from various schools in Leicester, 2000.

A group scene from this performance, Leicester, 2000.

Same as fig. 85.

Same as fig. 85.

Same as fig. 85.

Same as fig. 85.

IV Appendices

Nilima teaching a Kathak dance workshop for Irish dancers, 2002.

Nilima and two young Irish dancers, Leicester, 2002.

Nilima leading a Kathak dance workshop session for Irish dancers, 2002.

The Irish music ensemble accompanying the *Flaming Feet* performance, 2002.

IV Appendices

A scene from the award-winning *Flaming Feet* performance of Kathak and Irish Dance, 2002.

Same as fig. 94.

Nilima with Irish dancer Darren Mchale during a demonstration of *Flaming Feet* at Soar Valley College in Leicester, 2002.

IV   Appendices

Speech by David Soden at the Sinjini launch function, National Space Centre Leicester, 17 April 2007.

Speech by the Heritage Lottery Fund (HLF) chairman at the Sinjini launch function, 2007.

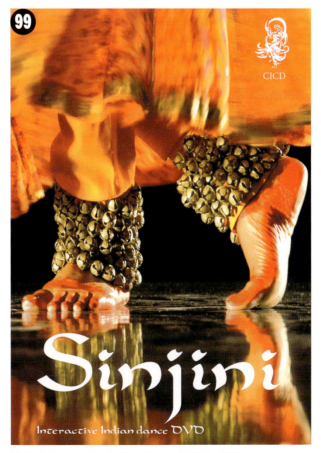

Sinjini (Interactive Indian Dance DVD), 2005.

IV   Appendices

Nilima's speech at the launch function.

Nilima's Kathak performance at the launch.

Nilima and the HLF chairperson at the launch.

IV   Appendices

Nilima and her family on a visit to the Yamada family from Kagoshima in London, 1994.

The Menski family during the visit of the Yamada family to Leicester, Christmas 1994.

The Yamada family on their Christmas visit to Leicester, 1994.

Christmas dinner with the Yamada family, 1994.

Mrs. Yamada and Nilima, 1994.

A family photos with the Yamada family, Christmas 1994 (nos. 103-108: reproduced with the permission of the Yamada family).

IV   Appendices

Nilima and a Japanese dancer, Tokyo, December 2003.

Nilima and Nalini Toshnival in Japan, December 2003.

Three Japanese dance students of Nalini Toshnival, Kobe, 2003.

IV   Appendices

Nalini Toshnival's Japanese students performing in the Sparkenhoe Theatre, Leicester, May 2004.

Same as fig. 112.

Same as fig. 112.

Nalini Toshnival working with her dance students, Sparkenhoe Theatre, May 2004.

Japanese students socialising with CICD students in the lounge at Churchill Street, 2004.

Japanese dance students having an Indian lunch at CICD, 2004.

IV   Appendices

The entrance corridor of CICD with historical fixtures from the earlier Polish butcher shop.

The CICD Noticeboard.

TV lounge and meeting room at CICD.

CICD's dance training and rehearsal studio at 50 Churchill Street, Leicester.

Same as fig. 121.

IV   Appendices

Entrance to the large CICD lounge.

CICD Exhibition Panel Boards celebrating 30 years of CICD, 2011.

Same as fig. 124.

Same as fig. 124.

Same as fig. 124.

119

IV   Appendices

CICD Board Meeting with Justy Barreto, Dr. Shashi Mehta, Christopher Maughan and Bela Zavery, March 2013.

CICD Board Meeting: Nilima and her husband.

CICD Board of Directors meeting March 2013: From left Justy Barreto, Dr. Shashi Mehta, Christopher Maughan, Bela Zavery, Aashish Parmar, Prof. Menski and Nilima. (nos. 118-39: photos by the editor).

IV   Appendices

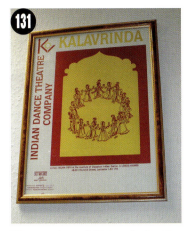

The poster of Kalavrinda, the Indian Dance Theatre Company, part of CICD's early dance development work, 1991.

The Outstanding Performance Award bagged by the CICD Youth Dance Group for performing an extract from the *Rainbow* performance, Derby, 1994.

The main poster of the *Rainbow* (*Indra Dhanush*) performances, 1995.

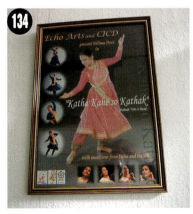

Nilima Devi's performance poster for *Katha Kahe so Kathak*, 1997.

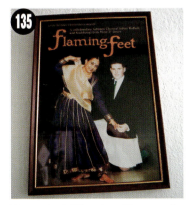

Poster of *Flaming Feet* performances with Nilima Devi and Darren Mchale, an Irish dancer, 2002.

IV Appendices

Poster for the Workshop of the Creative Partnership Project, 2004.

Kathak poster of Nilima Devi from the UK and Nalini Toshnival from Japan performing *Nrityam* ('Dance'), 2004.

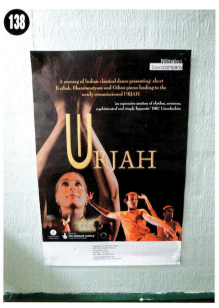

The poster for the *Urjah* performance, 2007.

Poster of *Flaming Feet*, Best Dance Performance Award, 2002.

IV Appendices

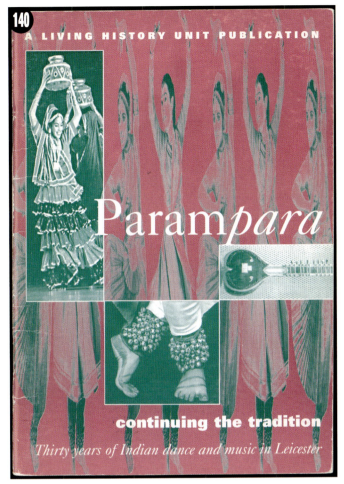

The *Parampara* book compiled by Colin Hyde, Smita Vadnerkar and Angela Cutting, Leicester, 1996.

Smita Vadnerkar and Colin Hyde at the launch of *Parampara* in Leicester, 1996.

IV Appendices

Karman: History of South Asian Dance in Leicester and Leicestershire by the Centre for Indian Classical Dance, 2012.

Appendix 5: Nilima Devi's MBE

Nilima Devi receiving her MBE from His Royal Highness Prince Charles, 7 June 2013 (nos. 1-3: reproduced with the permission of British Ceremonial Arts Limited).

IV   Appendices

Same as fig. 1.

Same as fig. 1.

IV   Appendices

Nilima Devi displaying her MBE, 7 June 2013.

Same as no. 4.

UK queen's honour for NRG danseuse

Vadodara-Born Nilima Devi Menski Awarded MBE

Prashant Rupera | TNN

Nilima Menski, after receiving her MBE medal from the Prince of Wales at an Investiture ceremony at Buckingham Palace

> Nilima Devi is married to Prof Werner Menski, a Sanskrit scholar and internationally renowned expert on Indian law at the University of London

Vadodara: Vadodara-born Nilima Devi Menski, the founder and artistic director of the Centre for Indian Classical Dance (CICD) in Leicester, and an overseas citizen of India, has been made Member of the Order of the British Empire (MBE). The 59-year-old danseuse figures in the Queen's New Year Honours List of 2013. She was formally given the MBE award by the Prince of Wales at a special ceremony held at Buckingham Palace in London on June 7.

Nilima Devi has been hounoured for her sustained contribution to the study and appreciation of Indian classical dance in the United Kingdom and abroad for over 30 years.

"I began my career in dance in Germany where I performed extensively in 1979 and 1980 before settling in the UK. In Leicester, which has a large population of people of Asian origin, there was no facility for learning Indian classical dance. Hence, in 1981, I started the Centre for Indian Classical Dance to teach people interested in classical Indian dance," Nilima Devi told TOI over phone.

She has also pioneered several programmes in association with public and private bodies for the study and appreciation of Indian arts in Britain.

She studied Kathak while studying for a Bachelors in Music. She completed Bachelors in Music in 1973 and Masters in Music in 1975 with distinction from Music College (now Faculty of Performing Arts, M S University) under Pandit Sunderlal Gangani.

"I am happy that I have been able to nurture over 20,000 students in Indian dance through teaching in British schools," said Nilima Devi. She has pioneered projects such as 'Sinjini' in 2009, a DVD on Indian music and dance that was produced with UK-based artistes and, in 2012, 'Karman', a book documenting the living history of the arts amongst the Indian diaspora.

She has also mentored accomplished British-born dance artistes such as Aakash Odedra, who recently toured with the British Council in India and performed 'Rising', a solo piece choreographed by Russell Maliphant, Sidi Larbi Cherkaoui and Akram Khan.

Nilima Devi is married to Prof Werner Menski, a Sanskrit scholar and internationally renowned expert on Indian law at the University of London. She has to her credit major productions such as the 'Ugly Duckling' in 1989, 'Triangle' in 1991, 'Rainbow' in 1993 and 'Urjah' in 2007, among others. These productions have made great strides towards transcending cultural and artistic barriers while retaining the spirit of Kathak dance.

The danseuse says that the major influences on her artistic and choreographic works have been late Pandit Durgalal from Delhi, Kumudini Lakhia from Ahmedabad and late Pandita Rohini Bate from Pune, who were also guest resident artistes at CICD.

From *Sunday Times of India*, Ahmedabad, July 14, 2013.

IV Appendices

Appendix 6: Dance posters and leaflets

The Ugly Duckling

Kathak Dance Drama by the Nilima Kathak Dance Company
Music composed by
Pandit Sundarlal Gangani and Pt. Vishvaprakash
Choreogragphy: Nilima Devi

Scene 1: The hatching of the eggs

Mother Duck is sitting on her nest. Then, four beautiful ducklings appear and explore their little world. The fifth egg takes a little longer to hatch, and when the fifth duckling finally appears, it is grey and ugly. The five ducklings enjoy life together, while Mother Duck is quite apprehensive about her ugly child. She leads them to the pond to test their swimming skills and finds that the ugly duckling is the best swimmer. Then she takes them all to the farmyard to show her family off. The other ducks, the geese and hens are highly suspicious about the Ugly Duckling, tease and trouble him, and finally chase him away from the yard.

Scene 2: The Ugly Duckling alone in the countryside

The Ugly Duckling wanders alone, sad and relieved at the same time, exploring the new environment. He sees a flock of ducks swimming on a lake, tries to befriend them, but they ignore him. He feels sad and neglected. Suddenly a loud shot from a hunter's gun and the ducks scatter. The Ugly Duckling hides in the grass, afraid of what will happen next.

Scene 3: "Even the dogs find me too ugly"

The hunter's dogs appear looking for a shot duck. They come close to the hidden Ugly Duckling, but do not touch him. He thinks he must be too ugly even for the dogs.

Scene 4: The old lady, her hen and cat meet the Ugly Duckling

The Ugly Duckling wanders around again and meets an old lady with her hen and cat. The old lady is happy to have a duck, expecting tasty eggs. But the hen and the cat are both very jealous, trouble the Ugly Duckling and make him leave.

Scene 5: The hard winter

Alone again, the Ugly Duckling feels winter coming and it starts to snow. He swims on a lake in circles, but the lake freezes and the Ugly Duckling gets stuck in the ice.

Scene 6: The farmer and his children

A farmer comes, picks up the Ugly Duckling from the ice and takes him home. The farmer's children gather round him, tease him and soon chase him around the house, making him leave.

1989/90

Nayana Whittaker
She started her classical dance training with Nilima Devi in 1982 and obtained her Diploma in Kathak from the Institute of Classical Indian Dance in 1989. She is now teaching folk, classical and creative dance at various community centres in Leicester and Loughborough. She has given many solo and group performances and has performed widely with Kalavrinda and with the Nilima Devi Kathak Dance Company.

Sushma Bhatt
She has been learning Kathak at the Institute of Classical Indian Dance in Leicester and has performed with Kalavrinda throughout the UK and at the Edinburgh Fringe Festival in 1990. A humanities graduate, she is planning to take an MA in Arts Administration and hopes to continue performing.

Jaimini Chauhan, Bhavita Jethwa and Dimple Zhaveri are three very young talented dancers, trained at the Institute of Classical Indian Dance from an early age. They are currently completing their Diploma in Kathak and have given many Kathak performances in community functions and various festivals. They have also taken part in folk dance performances with Kalavrinda and were the ducklings in the 1989 performances of The Ugly Duckling.

Acknowledgements

The Nilima Devi Kathak Dance Company would like to thank the following organisations and individuals for their kind support and help in making this production possible:

Leicester City Council, Leicestershire County Council , Raj and Company, the Asian Dance Support Group and the Institute of Classical Indian Dance for financial assistance.

Moat Community College, Knighton Fields Dance and Drama Centre and the Institute of Indian Classical Dance for the use of rehearsal space and facilities.

Rashmi Chhadha in Hounslow and Jenwill Printers in Leicester for visuals and publicity material.

Usha Mahenthralingam of Nottingham for the special backdrops for The Ugly Duckling and Loughborough College of Art and Design for designing the Ugly Duckling costumes.

Ian Whittaker and Paul Bull for video and technical assistance.

Last, but not least the parents of the children taking part in this performance for being wonderfully supportive and patient.

Nilima Devi

IV Appendices

Scene 7: The Ugly Duckling discovers his true identity

It is spring now, and the Ugly Duckling appears in a beautiful white coat. He sees another group of ducks on a pond, dancing full of joy, but they ignore him and he still feels unhappy and dejected. He flies away and, seeing his beautiful mirror image in the water, begins to wonder. Then he sees some very beautiful white birds swimming below him in the water and decides to join them. To his surprise they are very friendly and celebrate their meeting with a joyful dance.

Mother Duck: Nayana Whittaker
Ducklings: Hans Menski, Rakhee Solanki,
    Martin Menski, Binita Parmar
Ugly Duckling: Gita Lakhlani
Farmyard animals: Jagruti Gohil, Janita Raj, Sheetal Purohit,
    Swati Purohit, Bhavita Jethwa, Jaimini Chauhan
Ducks: Swati Purohit, Sheetal Purohit, Janita Raj,
    Cathy Doohar, Bijal Gokal, Rupali Chhatrisha
Dogs: Hans Menski, Martin Menski
Old lady: Nimisha Patel
Hen and cat: Rupali Chhatrisha, Hans Menski
Farmer: Nimisha Patel
Children: Jagruti Gohil, Rupali Chhatrisha
    Hans Menski, Martin Menski
Swans: Sushma Bhatt, Jaimini Chauhan, Bhavita Jethwa,
    Nimisha Patel, Shivani Watt, Nayana Whittaker,
    Dimple Zhaveri

INTERVAL

Contemporary Kathak
Music: Pandit Sundarlal Ganganî   Choreography: Nilima Devi

Invoking blessings: The opening dance focuses on Ganesha, the elephant-headed god, the remover of all obstacles. This piece is danced to a poem and elaborates the description of the various qualities of the elephant.

Dancers: Nilima Devi, Gita Lakhlani, Nayana Whittaker

Kite flying: Anyone who has ever taken part in the Indian kite flying festival, which is held in January in Gujarat and at other times of the year in different places, will particularly enjoy this dance item. The manifold preparations involve putting special paste on threads to make them stronger, making the kites and rolling up big balls of thread as supplies in the friendly battles with other kite flyers. The sky is full of kites and cries of joyful delight are heard as rival kites are cut and caught.

Dancers: Nilima Devi, Gita Lakhlani, Nayana Whittaker

Kathak Nritta

This is an abstract dance item based on the techniques of complicated rhythmic patterns, co-ordination of feet, graceful hands and body movements, various types of whirling movements, intricate hand gestures, movements of the limbs, eyes, eyebrows and neck movements. This piece was originally performed in 1988 and is now presented in a new choreography by Nilima Devi.

Dancers: Nilima Devi, Sushma Bhatt, Gita Lakhlani,
    Shivani Watt, Nayana Whittaker

Kathak on Beethoven: Piano Concerto No.1

This piece was originally choreographed by Nilima Devi as a solo item in 1984 and was widely performed to much acclaim. It is now presented in group choreography.

Dancers: Nilima Devi, Nimisha Patel, Shivani Watt

Major dancers of the Nilima Devi Kathak Dance Company

Gita Lakhlani
She completed her Diploma in Kathak at the Institute of Classical Indian Dance in Leicester in 1989 and has since continued to perform and teach Kathak dance. A lecturer by profession, she is also involved in conducting workshops and offers lecture demonstrations. After her debut performance with the Nilima Devi Kathak Dance Company in the "Triangle" in Autumn 1991, she is currently dancing the lead role in Hans Christian Andersen's Ugly Duckling.

Shivani Watt
Her interest in dance ranges from contemporary and jazz dance to Kathak. Since 1986 she has focused more on Kathak and Indian folk dancing. She has performed with the Kalavrinda Dance Company in productions at the Haymarket and Phoenix in Leicester and other venues, including the Edinburgh Fringe Festival in 1990. She is a final year BA student at London University and is teaching both Kathak and folk dance to young children.

Nimisha Patel
She is about to take the Diploma in Kathak at the Institute of Classical Indian Dance in Leicester and danced the lead role in an earlier production of The Ugly Duckling in 1989. Presently a student at Loughborough, training to be a maths teacher, she also took part in Leicester's pioneering Asian Dance Animateur Scheme and looks forward to teaching dance in the future. She has taken part in many performances with Kalavrinda, including the Edinburgh Fringe Festival.

IV Appendices

1994/5

INDRA DHANUSHA (Rainbow)

Dance production by
Nilima Devi Kathak Dance Company

Based on the philosophy of the Gita, an ancient Indian scripture whose message is timeless and universal, this is a new programme of Kathak dance.

The Gita's universal message is to experience oneness with the eternal, the Absolute, through one's chosen medium.

The dancers attempt to create this experience of oneness of humanity and divinity, presenting this theme in the form of North Indian classical Kathak dance with contemporary group choreography and creative music.

Choreography	Kumudini Lakhia
Dancers	Nilima Devi & Company
Music	Atul Desai
Lighting design	Bethan Evans

Nilima Devi is one of the leading Kathak exponents in the UK. She has trained many young dancers in Britain. Some of them are now actively involved in performing and teaching Indian dance at various community and educational establishments in the UK.

For further information please contact:
**Institute of Classical Indian Dance
48-50 Churchill Street
Leicester LE2 1FH
Phone (0533) 552862**

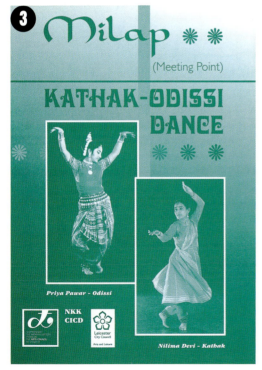

1994/5

Milap

NKK (CICD)

Nilmani Kathak Kendra, one of the foremost Kathak dance institutions in the UK, will be combining Kathak and Odissi, two distinct classical dance styles from India. The company will present a double bill performed by two of the most renowned dance exponents in Britain today – Nilima Devi (Kathak) and Priya Pawar (Odissi).

MILAP

MILAP weaves together rhythmic improvisations and mythological stories combined with spectacular expressive movements, choreographed in a duet form. 'Meeting Point' articulately illustrates the aesthetic distinctions between these two magical Indian classical dance styles.

Lighting Designer – Gerald Wells
Musicians – Vishwa Prakash, Baluji Shrivastava and Navinder Pal
Dancers – Priya Pawar and Nilima Devi

IV Appendices

5

ON: **SUNDAY**

30TH JUNE 1996

AT **7.30PM**

AT: **THE HAYMARKET THEATRE BELGRAVE GATE, LEICESTER**

TICKETS PRICES:

£7.00, £6.00, £5.00

(LESS £1 FOR LEISURE CARD AND STUDENTS)

TICKETS AVAILABLE FROM **HAYMARKET THEATRE**

TEL: 253 9797

A GALA EVENING OF *Indian* DANCE & MUSIC

With Sangeet Sabah and Community Indian Dance Groups in Leicester

THE EVENT IS JOINTLY PROMOTED BY THE ASIAN DANCE SUPPORT GROUP, LEICESTER CITY COUNCIL, LEICESTERSHIRE ARTS IN EDUCATION AND HAYMARKET THEATRE, WITH FINANCIAL SUPPORT FROM LEICESTER CITY COUNCIL AND LEICESTERSHIRE COUNTY COUNCIL

LEISURE SERVICES
Leicester City Council

1996

IV   Appendices

NILIMA DEVI KATHAK DANCE COMPANY

This Company was formed by Nilima Devi in 1990 with a view to promoting new and innovative solo and group choreography work in the Kathak style. The contemporary and creative themes explored by this Company display the many talents of Britain's first generation of Kathak dancers, who have been dedicated to Kathak for the last ten years.

Since 1990, the Company has performed all over Britain and has created a number of new Kathak dance productions, including 'The Triangle', 'The Ugly Duckling', and Kathak choreography with Western classical music. The *Leicester Mercury* hailed an earlier production of this dance company as "captivating". The *Nottingham Evening Post* praised the "graceful Indian movement" of their dances. The *Evening News* Edinburgh said that "Their movements were both intricate and stylised, requiring the utmost of them in concentration and synchronisation. Their costumes were as stunning as they were".

The Company is available to give full length performances, workshops, lecture-demonstrations, residencies and inset courses, and for project work in schools and colleges.

The performance fee of the company includes high quality publicity materials to help attract an audience.
★ 10" × 8" black and white photos.
★ A5 handbills.
★ Programme with notes about the performance and full biographies

Technical requirements
★ 9m × 9m performance space with a floor suitable for barefoot dance.
★ Plain backdrop, preferably black.
★ 6' × 12' raised platform for musicians, covered in a rug.
★ Variable number of high quality PA and mikes according to tour.
★ ²/₃ dressing rooms with mirrors; an iron and ironing board.
★ A general cover with spotlights for the musicians.

For further information please contact:
Rajesh Bhavsar at the Institute of Classical Indian Dance, 48 – 50 Churchill Street, Leicester LE2 1FH.
Tel: 0533 552862

1996

IV Appendices

KATHAK

Kathak is the most prominent classical dance style of Northern India. The word Kathak is derived from Sanskrit and relates to the telling of stories through mime and dance, thus referring to one main feature of this dance style. In traditional solo performances the dancer represents all the characters of a story through a rich repertoire of gestures, facial expressions and graceful movements of the limbs.

Kathak performances normally consist of two parts, nritta and nritya. The first, the so-called technical part, is a pure dance form focusing on technique, a tremendous sense of rhythm and joy of movement. The beauty of this part of Kathak lies, therefore, in the exact rendering of the rhythmic patterns, given by the instruments, through graceful body movements and the mystery of the artist's footwork. Nritya, the second element of Kathak performances, emphasises abhinaya, which is the explanation of a story or a song through mime, gestures of the hands and symbolic postures of the body. In the Kathak style, this is not rigid and allows the artist to use a variety of free movements, thus leaving

interpretation of a story or poem and rhythmic improvisations greatly to the artist's power of imagination and creativity. The stories performed in Kathak come from different types of Indian literature, the oldest being probably from the great epics Ramayana and Mahabharata. Many stories and songs of medieval origin are in praise of Lord Krishna.

NILIMA DEVI

Nilima Devi is a highly qualified Kathak artist from India and is now one of the most respected pioneers of Indian dance development in Europe. Trained at the famous Music College of M. S. University Baroda, under the guidance of Pandit Sundarlal Gangani, she went to Germany in 1979 and then moved to Britain in 1980. She has been running the Institute of Classical Indian Dance in the city of Leicester since 1981.

Nilima Devi has given many solo performances in India, Germany and Britain and has been praised for her graceful interpretations of Kathak stories and her experimental work with European classical music and with group choreography. In Britain, she has trained many Kathak students in her Institute, which provides a six-year Diploma course in Kathak. The first two students completed their Diploma in 1988, and another four are close to completion.

Since 1985, Nilima Devi has also worked in various capacities to promote and establish a pioneering project for Asian dance development in Britain. Her educational work in Leicester includes training youth and adult dance groups, in-service training for teachers, and many workshops in schools and colleges, contributing to multicultural education. She has also invited many dance artists to Leicester to enhance the community development of Asian dance.

134

IV   Appendices

1997/98

135

IV Appendices

5. TIPPANI AND BEDLA - Folk dances of Saurashtra and Gujerarat. Tippani are wooden sticks used to level the floor surface during building. Female workers express joy through the dance with the rhythmic use of sticks. Bedla is a celebration of the harvest performed at village fairs using clapping and miming with dancers carrying water pots.

Dancers: Jaine Pancholi, Rina Bhakta, Punam Varia, Darshana Mistry, Pooja Patel, Anusha Patel, Khyati Bhavsar, Hetal Patel, Rachana Kotecha, Manisha Patel, Bhavika Patel, Veena Parmar, Rina Patel, Anisha Rajput.

Direction: Vaidehi Pancholi

Group: Woodgate Resource Centre & Bhagini Centre

6. GHUMMAR - a folk dance from Rajasthan performed by women during marriage, social and Navrati festivities using circular movements, mime and graceful hand movements.

Dancers: Hemali Patel, Nayan Whittaker, Kundand Patel, Priti Raithatha.

Direction: Dancers

INTERVAL

SANGHEET SABHA

1. Kathak dance piece set to Tal Tin Tal - Dhrut Laya.

Dancers: Bejal Bhula, Krupa Parmar, Resha Patel, Anjali Champaneria, Bejal Devalia, Sita Patel, Mira Modi, Kesha Raithatha

Direction: Nilima Devi

2. Classical singing Rag-Malkauns-Tal-Tintal.

Singers: Sharu Sharma, Roopal Bathia, Rajeshwari Gor

Tabla Accompaniment: Bhinderjeet Singh

Direction: Surinder Singh

3. Tabla playing Tal - Jhaptal, set to ten beat time cycle.

Participants: Hitesh Prajapati, Shyam Patel, Dipesh Pankhaniya, Rajesh Singh, Anish Raja, Ravi Ravji

Direction: Gurmeet Singh

FOLK DANCES OF INDIA performed by various community groups.

1. GIDDHA - graceful Panjabi folk dance performed by women only at marriage ceremonies and social gatherings.

Dancers: Nimisha Parmar, Vaidehi Pancholi, Kundan Patel, Priti Raithatha, Nayana Whittaker, Hemali Patel.

Direction, singing and Dholki playing: Gurjeet Johal.

Group: Community Dance Tutors

2. SUPADA (vessel for cleaning grain in India) - a folk dance from Gujarat performed with Supada.

Dancers: Vanisha Mistry, Sital Kavia, Jaimini Mistry, Bindiya Mistry, Nikita Chavla, Shallani Anand.

Direction: Nayana Whittaker

Group: Sanatan Community Project

3. TRIBAL DANCE - energetic folk dance with natural grace performed by tribes living in hilly areas in India.

Dancers: Poonam Lakhani, Arti Bhatt, Sonal Pala, Kesha Raithatha, Amisha Bhagwan, Deepa Sarmàn, Parul Kurji, Yashodhara Pandya, Anjana Gohel, Krupa Tahna, Rupal Patel

Direction: Priti Raithatha

Group: Rusheymead Secondary School

4. SANTHAL - a folk dance from Bihar performed by Adivasis based on the theme of nature and social customs.

Dancers: Sujata Mistry, Bhavika Mistry, Bhavini Gohil, Sabina Sulemanji, Tejal Mistry, Jeamini Mistry, Urvashi Odedra, Jaimini Mistry.

Direction: Priya Pawar.

Group: Sanatan Community Project

IV Appendices

KATHAK
Nilima Devi

As a Choreographer

Nilima Devi has choreographed countless solo traditional Kathak pieces for her students and many new pieces presenting group choreography, often in the form of dance-drama, some leading to major performances. The main productions are 'Kathak Katha' in 1990, 'The Ugly Duckling' (1990, 1992), 'Triangle' (1992), and she produced the award-winning 'Rainbow' programme in 1993-94 with choreography by Kumudini Lakhia.

As part of the annual Leicestershire Schools Festivals, she has choreographed many dance productions at Leicester's prestigious Haymarket Theatre, such as 'Aladdin' (1993), 'Stars and Stripes' (1994), 'Dance Spectular' (1995), 'Kathak Tarana' for an Evening of Indian Dance (1996) and a section from 'Rainbow' for the celebration of 20 years of Youth Dance in Leicester (1997). Her most recent production is 'Kathak Sargam', presented in the Asian Dance and Music Gala evening at the Phoenix Theatre in May 1997.

For further information please contact:
Rajesh Bhavsar at the Center for Indian Classical Dance,
48-50 Churchill Street, Leicester LE2 1 FH.
Tel.: 0116 2552862

1998

are now teaching and performing at community and school level within the Midlands region and in London.

Two of her students, Shivani Satya and Nimisha Patel, have been awarded the National scholarships of Aditi in 1994 and 1995 to study full-time for one year in India at the Kadamb Institute in Ahmedabad.

Since 1985, Nilima Devi has worked in various capacities to establish a pioneering project for Asian dance development in Britain. Her educational work as a teacher in Leicester includes training youth and adult dance groups, in-service training for teachers and many workshops in schools and colleges, contributing to multicultural education.

She also works as an Advisor for South Asian dance development for Leicestershire Arts and has established a consistent training project for

talented school children, who receive systematic training in Kathak dance from the age of eight years onwards. The fruits of that work are now, several years later, beginning to show in a series of excellent showcase performances by these young dancers.

For the past few years the role of the Nilmani Kathak Kendra has changed. It has now become a centre for advanced Kathak and examination training, as well as solo performance training for devoted and talented students of Kathak dance.

IV Appendices

KATHAK

Kathak is the most prominent classical dance style of Northern India. The word Kathak is derived from Sanskrit and relates to the telling of stories through mime and dance, thus referring to one main feature of this dance style. In traditional solo performances the dancer represents all the characters of a story through a rich repertoire of gestures, facial expressions and graceful movements of the limbs.

Kathak performances normally consist of two parts, nritta and nritya. The first, the so-called technical part, is a pure dance form focussing on technique, a tremendous sense of rhythm and joy of movement. The beauty of this part of Kathak lies, therefore, in the exact rendering of the rhythmic patterns, given by the instruments, through graceful body movements and the mystery of the artist's footwork.

Nritya, the second element of Kathak performances, emphasises abhinaya, which is the explanation of a story or a song through mime, gestures of the hands and symbolic postures of the body. In the Kathak style, this is not rigid and allows the artist to use a variety of free movements, thus leaving interpretation of a story or poem and rhythmic improvisations greatly to the artist's power of imagination and creativity. The stories performed in Kathak come from different types of Indian literature, the oldest being probably from the great epics Ramayana and Mahabharata. Many stories and songs of medieval origin are in praise of Lord Krishna.

Nilima Devi
North Indian Classical Dancer

Training

Nilima Devi is a fully-trained, accomplished dancer. She completed a Masters degree (MMus) in Kathak dance from the Faculty of Performing Arts, M. S. University, Baroda, the famous Baroda Music College, with distinction. She studied under the guidance of Narendra Patel, Prafulla Oza and Pandit Sunderlal Gangani. During her training, she also took part in a choreography course organised by the cultural department of Gujarat Natya Sangit Samiti in Ahmedabad, led by Maya Rao.

As a promising Kathak student, Nilima Devi won Government scholarships throughout her training. She was also awarded a National Scholarship from Delhi Kathak Kendra in 1973 to receive further training in Delhi. During her training, Nilima Devi gave many solo Kathak performances for dance festivals in Gujarat and Bombay and played a leading role in some dance ballets.

"One never stops learning". This philosophy has encouraged Nilima Devi to receive guidance and assistance from many great Kathak artists, such as Pandit Durgalal and Padmashree Kumudini Lakhiya. She will continue to work with other professional Kathak maestros and artists from other dance traditions. This will help to develop Kathak dance in a broader context.

"A young promising Kathak dancer of Gujarat"
Lokasatta, Baroda.

Performance

As a professional Kathak dancer, Nilima Devi has performed in many places in Gujarat, in Bombay and elsewhere in India. In 1979-80 she gave sixteen solo Kathak performances throughout Germany and was praised for her graceful interpretations of Kathak stories.

Since 1981 she has been performing solo Kathak programmes for various occasions locally and nationally in the UK. As part of her work as a Dance Animateur since 1984, she has performed in hundreds of schools and many community organisations throughout the East Midlands to raise the profile and awareness of Kathak dance.

In 1989, she created a solo work, 'Kathak Katha' with the help of her Guru, Pandit Sunderlal Gangani, which was performed in various places in the Midlands and London.

As a solo dancer, Nilima Devi has performed for various national and international festivals in the UK. Her solo Kathak piece on Beethoven's Piano Concerto No. 1 was filmed by "Here and Now."

"A captivating performer" enthused and Leicester Mercury. The Nottingham Evening Post praised the "graceful Indian movement".

As a Teacher

After her Masters degree in Kathak, Nilima started teaching in Baroda and then in Germany (Tagore Institute, Bonn; Dortmund Ballet School and Bochum), creating lot of interest for Kathak dance in Germany.

In 1981, she founded the Nilmani Kathak Kendra in Leicester and has taught hundred of students, some of whom have managed to study up to Diploma level in Kathak dance. Some of them were subsequently trained as dance animateurs and

138

9

LEICESTERSHIRE COUNTY COUNCIL
EDUCATION DEPARTMENT
ARTS IN EDUCATION

Leicester City Council

Arts in Education

PROGRAMME DIRECTORS

Sangeet Sabha
Ramnik Varu - Vocal/Harmonium
Surinder Singh Sond - Vocal
Gurmit Singh Virdee - Tabla
Tirlok Singh - Sitar
Nilima Devi - Kathak Dance

Community Dance Tutors
Priti Raithatha - Rushey Mead School
Vadehi Pancholi - Woodgate Resource Centre
Nimisha Parmar - Belgrave Neighbourhood Centre

ARTS IN EDUCTION SANGEET SABHA

Vocal (Singing)
Roopal Bathia, Yogesh Bali, Sneh Hazari, Vaishali Kalidas, Asha Mashru, Deepa Mashru, Niveta Muman, Primal Kotecha

Tabla
Bhinderjeet Singh, Hans Menski, Nitin Odedra, Ravi Ravji, Rajesh Singh, Dipesh Pankhania, Shyam Patel, Anish Raja, Mehul Somani, Deepa Maisuria, Dipesh Maisuria, Amit Mistry, Jaykishen Patel, Dhruv Upadhya, Savraj Sokhi

Sitar
Bhavini Gohil, Rohit Blall, Arachna Blall, Rupinder Kaur Waiwala

1998

LEICESTERSHIRE & LEICESTER ARTS IN EDUCATION

PRESENTS

A CELEBRATION OF DIWALI

FRIDAY 16TH OCTOBER 1998

Victorian Picture Gallery
Leicester Museum,
New Walk, Leicester

IV   Appendices

~ PROGRAMME ~

(1) **Diva Dance**
Creative dance signifying Festival of Light based on Bhajan describing glory of God Rama.
Lyrics from literature Tulsi Ramayan.
Kathak Dancers
Kishan Gandhi, Durga Gandhi, Asha Mistry, Shivani Patel, Jaina Patel

(2) **Vocal**
Aarti of "Maa Jagdamba"
based on Raga Yaman in Tal Kaherwa
Composition by Hridaynath Mangeshkar
Lyric by Pandit Narrendra Sharma

Vocal : Khayal
Raga Bhimpalasi in Tintal Madhya Laya

(3) **Sitar**
Rag Yaman in Tintal (16 beats)

Sitar
Rag Hamir in Tintal

(4) **Tabla**
Tintal (16 beats)
Kayada Ajrara Style,
Paltas and Chakkar Dhar Tihai

~ INTERVAL ~

(5) **Vocal**
Devotional Song
set to 8 beat cycle - Tal Kaherwa

(6) **Tabla Ensemble in Tintal (16 beats)**
An effort to integrate three teams of players with differing age patterns and performance abilities to render a high powered group performance with astonishing variety

(7) **Kathak Dance based on "Shivastrota"**
Sangeet Sabha Kathak Dancers
Lyrics by Ravan

Anjali Champaneria, Bejal Bhula, Sita Patel, Akash Odedra, Lisa Surti, Bejal Devalia, Resha Patel

(8) **Bharatnatyam Dance based on Shiva Sloka from Abhinaya Darpanam and Ganesh Purana**
Belgrave Neighbourhood Centre Group

Neha Chauhan, Nidhidha Gohil, Urvi Taank, Shreya Parmar

(9) **Dance based on Lord Krishna story**
Lyrics by Narsinh Mehta
Woodgate Resource Centre Group

Anusha Patel, Jaine Pancholi, Rina Bhakta, Garima Rathod, Khyati Bhavsar, Punam Varia, Puja Patel, Darshna Mistry, Hetal Patel, Namita Patel

(10) **Indian Dance based on Mira Bhajan**
Rushey Mead School

Mira Khakhadia, Krishna Patel, Kavita Karsan, Kesha Raithatha, Kavita Rajyaguru, Alpa Jungi, Pooja Khunti, Krupa Tanna, Sapna Patel, Rupal Patel, Rachna Makwana, Shamim Razakmm, Rupa Devani, Sharazad Khoshla, Vishba Prapajapati, Misha Chandarana, Milli Bhojani

(11) **Kathak Dance in 10 beat cycle based on Tal Jhaptal**
Sangeet Sabha Kathak Dancers

Jagruti Gohil, Sheetal Purohit, Swati Purohit, Rupali Chhatrisha

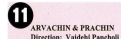

ARVACHIN & PRACHIN
Direction: Vaidehi Pancholi

Dancers: Veena Parmar, Rina Patel, Neha Dave, Puja Patel, Darshna Mistry, Jaine Pancholi, Anusha Patel, Rina Bhakta, Hetal Patel, Garima Rathod, Punam Varia, Anisha Rajput

Group: Asian Dance Development Unit & Bhagini Centre

ARVACHIN
Direction: Hemali Patel

Dancers: Hemali Patel, Lisa Surti, Swati Purohit, Sheetal Purohit, Jagruti Gohil, Rupali Chhatresha, Bejal Devalia, Bejal Bhula

Group: Knighton Fields Centre Kathak Group

••

ACKNOWLEDGEMENTS

LEICESTERSHIRE COUNTY COUNCIL
Chair: Mrs Cordelia Brock
Director of Education: Jackie Strong

LEICESTER CITY COUNCIL
Leader: Sir Peter Soulsby
Director of Arts & Leisure: Mike Gallagher
Head of Arts & Entertainments: Mike Candler

ARTS IN EDUCATION
Service Manager: Peter Baker
Head of Performance: Catherine Hutchon

LEICESTER CITY COUNCIL
ARTS ADVISORY
ASIAN COMMUNITY DANCE GROUPS

&

LEICESTERSHIRE & LEICESTER
ARTS IN EDUCATION
SANGEET SABHA

(Arts in Education: A Joint Leicestershire County
Council & Leicester City Council Service)

presents

VIVIDH

ASIAN DANCE
&
MUSIC SHOWCASE

at

PHOENIX ARTS

SUNDAY 21ST MARCH 1999
7.30 P.M.

1999

PROGRAMME

SANGEET SABHA

VOCAL

HYMN from Rig Ved – composed in Raga Deshkar followed by a group song from Udiya region of India (song composed in Raga Sarang)

Vocal Ensemble: Yogesh Bali, Roopal Bathia, Asha Mashru, Navita Muman, Ricky Modi, Deepa Mashru, Primal Kotecha, Arjun Singh. Tabla: Bhinderjit Singh

KHAYAL – Raga Kalavati by Roopal Bathia & Yogesh Bali
Direction: Ramnik Varu & Surinder Singh

Tabla: Bhinderjit Singh

TABLA

TAL-TEEN-TAL - 16 Beats/Raga Sohini starts with Peshkar, Kayada, Rela and ends with a complex set of Ti-Hai's.

LAHERA by Roopal Bathia
Direction: Gurmeet Singh

Tabla Ensemble: Mehul Somani, Dipesh Rankani, Ravi Ravji, Anesh Raja, Shyam Patel, Dipa Measuria, Dipesh Measuria, Amit Mistry, Kartar Singh, Dhruv Upadhyay, Savraj Sokhi, Bhindarjit Neer, Hans Menski, Niten Odedra, Jaykishan Patel

SITAR

LIGHT DHUN – Raga Pahadi

Sitar Ensemble: Rohit Ballal, Archana Ballal, Rupinder Kaur

SITAR VADAN - Raga Gara by Bhavini Gohil
Direction: Tirlok Singh

Tabla: Bhinderjit Singh

TARANA – Kathak dance piece composed to an abstract musical composition blended with rhythmic improvisation in Taal-Tintal.
Direction: Nilima Devi

Dancers: Lisa Surti, Swati Purohit, David Miodrag, Rupali Chhatresha, Sheetal Purohit, Jagruti Gohil, Akash Odedra, Hans Menski, Bejal Devalia, Vibhuti Chauhan, Bejal Bhula, Krupa Parmar, Kesha Raithatha, Deepa Mashru, Alpa Yungi

INTERVAL

SOUTH ASIAN DANCE (COMMUNITY GARBA DANCES)

PRACHIN
Direction: Nimisha Parmar

Dancers: Shreya Parmar, Mona Valand, Shruti Chauhan, Neha Chauhan, Urvi Tank, Ishwari Arya, Nidhita Gohil, Trishna Sharma

Group: Asian Dance Development Unit

ARVACHIN
Direction: Nayana Whittaker

Dancers: Jaiminee Mistry, Sujata Parmar, Bhavini Gohil, Sangita Mistry, Rina Babla, Hema Acharya, Shallini Anand, Nikita Chawla

Group: Shri Sanatan Community Project

ARVACHIN
Direction: Priti Raithatha

Dancers: Dhara Pandya, Kesha Raithatha, Krupa Tanna, Reena Chauhan, Rachna Makwani, Rupa Devani, Rupal Patel, Sapna Patel, Shameem Razak, Yashodara Pandya

Group: Rusheymead Secondary School & ICSAD

IV Appendices

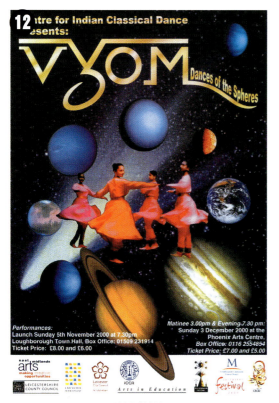

1999/2000

IV Appendices

National KATHAK DANCE Conference

Thursday 29 June 2000

LEICESTERSHIRE & LEICESTER ARTS IN EDUCATION, KNIGHTON FIELDS CENTRE

Herrick Road
Leicester

CONTACT INFORMATION

SADHANA VAIDYA
Centre for Indian Classical Dance
50-46 Churchill Street
Leicester
LE2 1FH

tel: 0116 255 2862
fax: 0116 285 4472
email: cicd@menski.demon.co.uk

2000

13 BOOKING FORM

FEES:
(including vegetarian lunch and refreshments)
£30 students and dancers
£50 community organisations and charities
£75 statutory independent and private sector

**Please make cheques payable to C.I.C.D.
Send with the completed form below to:**

SADHANA VAIDYA
Centre for Indian Classical Dance
50-46 Churchill Street
Leicester,
LE2 1FH

tel: 0116 255 2862
fax: 0116 285 4472
email: cicd@menski.demon.co.uk

Name
Company
Address

Postcode
Telephone
Fax
email

I would like to book:
  x student/dancer places
  x community organisation/charity places
  x statutory independent/private places

IV Appendices

KATHAK DANCE IN BRITAIN

This national conference has been organised by:

- The Centre for Indian Classical Dance, Leicester
- Arts & Cultural Services, Leicester City Council
- Leicestershire & Leicester Arts in Education

The aims of the conference are:

- To consider the past, present and future direction of Kathak dance teaching in the UK within the wider context of dance developments
- To bring together dance practitioners, educationalists and academics, as well as representatives of schools, local authorities, community organisations and funding bodies
- To provide a platform for debate about South Asian dance development in the UK, with special reference to Kathak
- To increase the academic profile of South Asian dance studies in the UK and to address a deficit of discussion in this field
- To provide a platform for young dancers and dance practitioners to participate in these discussions
- To increase the profile of Leicester & Leicestershire as pioneering local authorities in facilitating South Asian dance provisions in schools and in the community.

PLANNED PROGRAMME FOR THE DAY

09.30	Registration, coffee/tea and exhibition
10.00	Introductions; Peter Baker, Werner Menski
10.15	Social inclusion and the arts: Keynote address Naseem Khan [Arts Council of England]
10.35	Kathak past, present and future in the UK: A national overview presented by Reginald Massey
10.55	Kathak dance in the UK: A practitioners perspective from Nilima Devi
11.15	Questions to all three speakers
11.35	Tea break
12.00	**Discussion Groups:** 1. Kathak as a non-indigenous dance form in the UK: A case of social exclusion? [Dr. Werner Menski] 2. Kathak artists in the UK as educators [Sushmita Ghosh and Nilima Devi] 3. Kathak dance in the British School Curriculum. Is Kathak training worth the effort? [Sushma Mehta] 4. Kathak in Higher Education [Professor Christopher Bannerman] 5. Dance NVQ's and life-long learning [Ruth Churchill] 6. Dancers and musicians: Need for mutual support? [Dharambir Singh]
12.45	Feedback from discussion groups

13.00	Lunch and exhibition
14.00	Panel discussion on dance(r) education and Kathak in formal education systems **Panelists:** David Henshaw [ISTD], Sujata Banerjee [Kadam], Gauri Sharma [ISTD]. Dr. Frances Shepherd [Prayag Sangit Samiti], Shanti Nagaraja [ADiTi], Pratap Pawar [Triveni]
14.45	Panel discussion on support for Kathak dance(rs) in informal education contexts **Panelists:** Joy Foxley [teacher and story teller], Enelli Hanson [Akademi], Vina Ladwa [Manushi], Gopa Nath [Surtal Asian Arts], Steve White [Head, Rushey Mead School].
15.30	Tea break
15.45	**Plenary session:** Action plan for the future issues arising during the day and future tasks
16.00	Kathak performance
16.30	Close of conference

IV Appendices

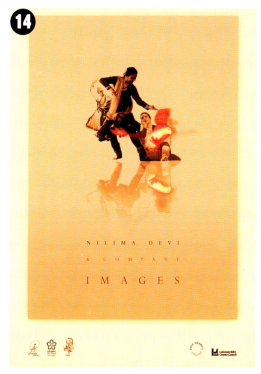

2001

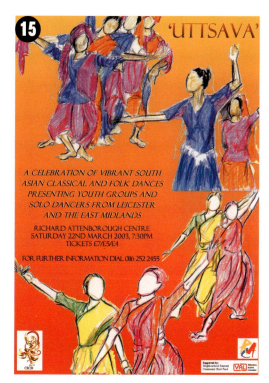

2003

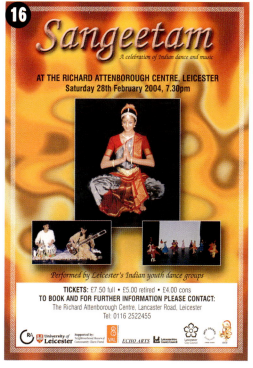

2004

IV Appendices

What is the state of dance today? Is it a marriage of techniques, cultures and styles, or do we need to look at dance and its different approaches and traditions separately?

Well that's what these seminars hope to do, explore the role of dance in Leicester and the region, and its international connections.

Serious about Dance? Let's Talk is a seminar series focused on African Caribbean, Asian, community dance and dance and disability. With speakers such as leading Caribbean intellectual Professor Rex Nettleford, Tanusree Shankar, the Kolkata based, internationally renowned exponent of the Shankar Technique, Sue Rosenbloom of local dance company Anima Dance and Rachel Freeman of celebrated dance company Blue Eyed Soul, the seminars will provide an environment for many different perspectives which will be reported in the final seminar report published by the Peepul Centre.

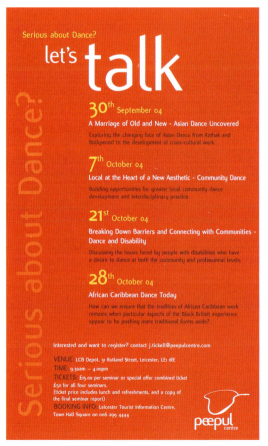

2004

IV   Appendices

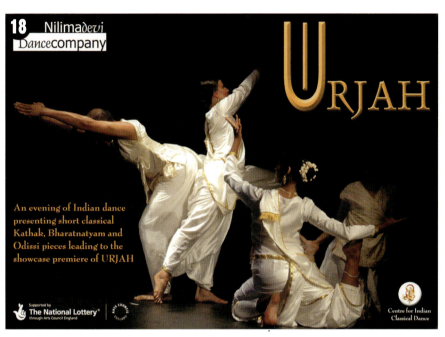

2005

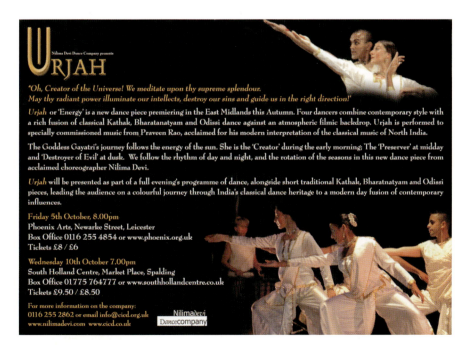

IV   Appendices

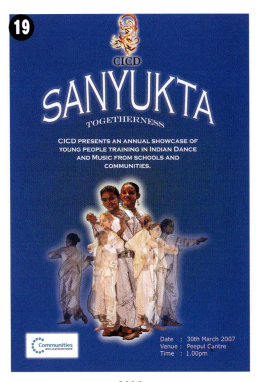

2006

Sanyukta presents the Annual Showcase of young people training at various schools after hours and at community centres, since September 2006

This Matinee Showcase presents nearly 100 young people in Indian Classical, Folk, creative and Bollywood dance styles and Music taught by professional instructors of CICD (The Centre for Indian Classical Dance)

Funded by Connecting Communities, this project aims to develop understanding and appreciation between different cultures through teaching of Indian dance and music after school hours and at various community centres to young people.

The project is co-ordinated by Akash Odedra, the Staff of CICD and project director NILIMA DEVI. This annual showcase is free for school children, their parents, school staff and people from the community who wish to attend the performance.

The students performing will be from the following schools and community centres:

Ravenhurst ✓	Belgrave Neighbourhood Centre
Fernvale ✓	Shree Hindu Mandir
Catherine Juniors ✓	CICD
Shaftesbury Primary	(Centre for Indian Classical Dance)
Satya Sai School	
Abbey Primary ✓	
Highfields Primary ✓	

Venue : Peepul Centre
TIME : 1PM to 2.45PM
Admission : FREE
For further information contact CICD on
0116 2552862
Info@cicd.org.uk

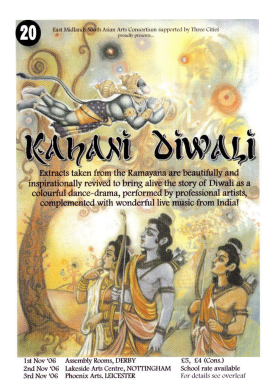

2006

IV   Appendices

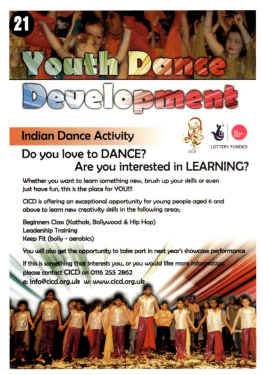

2006

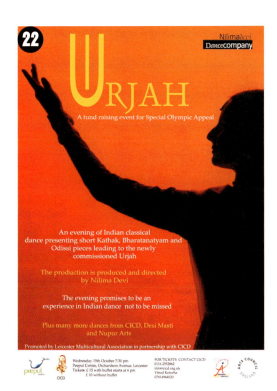 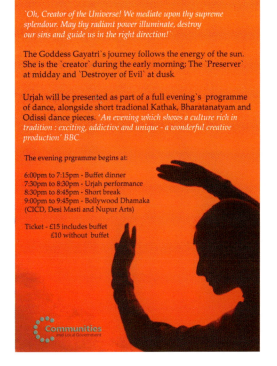

2007

IV   Appendices

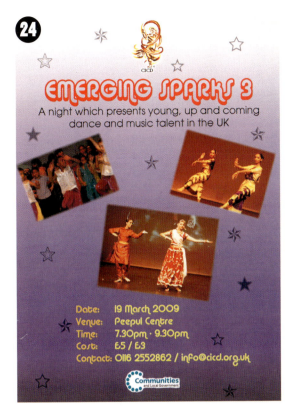

IV Appendices

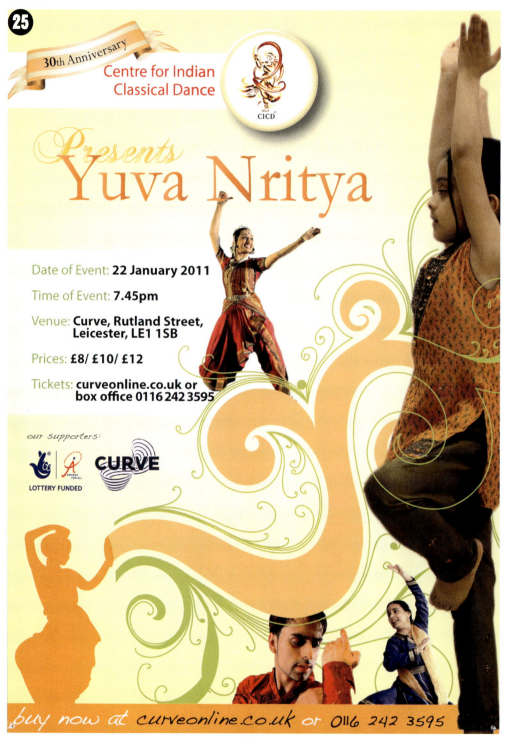

2011

IV Appendices

2011

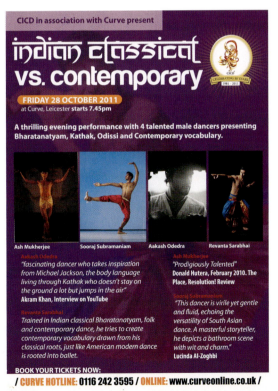

IV Appendices

Appendix 7: Memories by Nilima Devi's students

Training in Kathak since childhood and becoming a performer

I spent my early childhood in Birmingham, where I was born in 1984. From a young age, I was somewhat obsessed with dance and deeply interested in religious/spiritual and cultural issues. My world began to revolve around dance, as I learnt more and more about gods and goddesses and their heroic deeds and saw this put into the medium of exciting films. I used to mimic film dances, with my family as sort of amused onlookers. In my day-to-day routines, each movement began to be subconsciously choreographed.

We moved to Leicester when I was eight. One day my father brought me the phone number of Nilima Devi, which he had got from listening to the local Sabras Radio. I guarded this number jealously and soon my mother rang to enquire about the possibility of me taking dance classes. I was called for an audition and soon went in my school uniform to Churchill Street, where the dance teacher was in the studio with her younger son. He first demonstrated some Kathak moves and then played the tabla while I showed off my dance skills, performing my favourite film dance item by copying Hema Malini. To my relief, Nilima Devi detected a good sense of rhythm and potential and agreed to teach me. So at the age of eight, I commenced formal training in Kathak at the Centre of Indian Classical Dance (CICD) and quickly began to relish this.

I soon transferred to the Knighton Fields Dance and Drama Centre, where Nilima Devi was then teaching several classes on Saturdays. Every Friday night, I got very excited, as Saturday virtually meant that Christmas had come, every week for the next few years! What a buzzing place, with orchestral music, both Western and Indian, drama, ballet, contemporary dance and of course our Kathak classes. I sneaked in early to see other groups practise and delayed my leaving, cherishing every moment in that inspiring environment. I was eager to use *ghungroos*, the dancing bells, which only advanced students were allowed to wear. Indeed I was soon among those advanced students and before I could blink, became involved in performances, too. One of my initial roles was as one of Krishna's friends in *Kaliya Daman*, the story of the big ferocious snake subdued by little Krishna, my teacher's younger son. We also performed in *The Ugly Duckling* and I really enjoyed the *Stars and Stripes* piece in 1994 (*American Dream*), in which we were Native Americans battling for our land.

These early performances gave me a taste for the stage and began to shape my outlook on performing as I became addicted to the euphoria of being on stage with others, creating an enjoyable piece together. *The Jungle Book*, a show at the Haymarket Theatre Main House in Leicester in 1995, provided a first opportunity to help choreograph, when I was barely eleven. Because our teacher had suddenly been hospitalised, her two sons and I faced the responsibility to set up a major performance involving forty dancers. We had the music and now made up creative moves as we went along, with one week to go. Taking the role of Moogly, I discovered the pleasure of bringing a vision to life, together with Balu the bear and Bagheera, the panther. This thrilling team spirit was again present in the dramatically rhythmic *Tarana* performance of 1996.

Initially I did not like performing as a soloist and preferred creative teamwork. Taking exams from year to year was useful for confidence building and also involved learning more about theory and aesthetics. This varied training increased my versatility as a dancer and helped me to pass all six years of the Imperial Society for the Teachers of Dance (ISTD) Diploma in Kathak. In the process, my sense of spirituality changed and became more holistic over time. On the dance floor, I always enjoyed creating my own movements by combining elements from different dance styles. I guess because my early teachers knew that I was learning other styles as well, it was a nice excuse for me to be just that little extra-creative. Most significantly, working with very different choreographers later completely changed my relationship to space. In traditional Kathak, this is much more grounded, while in my present dance this depends on the piece and the performance environment, with everything becoming much more fluid. Today's modern versions of contemporary Kathak are still about stories and are still communicating something, but we do so in a quite different way from before, not the least because there is now a global audience.

My first major solo performance was in a big arena in Mumbai and then in Pune, where Nilima Devi had taken me in 2000 to learn from famous Kathak dancers and prepare CICD's Millennium performance of *Vyom: The Dance of the Spheres*. After that I trained in several other dance styles, not only Bharatnatyam as before, but now also Indo-Jazz, Contemporary Dance and some ballet. My most significant decision was to travel to India repeatedly to work with different teachers and choreographers, building on my solid foundations in Kathak. Especially important for me was the Ekatra project, a Kathak and contemporary dance piece choreographed by Kumudini Lakhia and Filip Van Huffel, which I performed at the Royal Opera House and Sadler's Wells Theatre in London. Most memorable was the 2004 training at the Shiamak Davar Institute for Performing Arts (SDIPA) in Mumbai. In 2006, I began to work all over the UK and in December that year performed Kathak and contemporary dance in Paris alongside Sonia Sabri. Performances in Canada followed, on three separate occasions. More recent work, again in Leicester, included *Samyukta* ('Togetherness') in 2006, where I choreographed various dance pieces for eighty students, while *Emerging Sparks* at the Peepul Centre in Leicester (2007) was an important springboard for upcoming professional dancers.

My father had not really been involved in these dance activities, but was always there when I needed him. My grandmother, too, gave me space to just do what I wanted to do when it came to dance. Once I developed my first major solo show, *Rising*, which by now I have performed 178 times all over the world, my father came to the premiere and has been much more involved ever since.

Rising was a key experience in my career as a soloist in several ways. We had secured

IV   Appendices

the support of Akram Khan as my mentor for a dance piece of ten minutes. None of us was satisfied with such a short piece, so we involved the leading contemporary choreographers Sidi Larbi Cherkaoui and Russell Maliphant, who saw something in me worth developing. Initially lost in that new style of working in cutting-edge contemporary dance, my sense of space changed yet again and these choreographers had a huge impact on my artistic work and vision. I began to experience that a premiere show is a special moment, but one has to let the project grow. It has to become a part of you and you have to make it breathe in your own soul. Other personal inputs in my artistic work relate to the memory of my grandmother's tattoo marks (*Ink*) and the very personal experience of dyslexia (*Murmur*), a Double Bill which by now I have performed more than eighty times.

As my relationship to dance and to being a performer has gradually changed, I am beginning to read more now and am seeking to develop different lenses for presenting artistic dance-related work. I see myself in future working more on choreography, or maybe in curating roles, or in documentation. The dancer's soul-mind-body connection continues to fascinate me. From the beginnings of a small boy crazy about dance, I have developed and matured through periods of adolescence and young adulthood, becoming enriched on the way as a person, more able to present my work to varied audiences, thus constantly rebalancing my own position when I find myself on a stage. I go back to my first teacher, Nilima Devi, from time to time and remain in touch with her two sons, who do so very different things from me now. Yet my life trajectory, too, has taken me outside of Leicester and has made me more of a citizen of the world. My roots are still partly in Leicester, but my personal and spiritual experience, fortified by being a performer on stage, is connecting me to the globe and the universe, as well as my constantly changing and varied audiences all over the world.

Aakash Odedra
20 March 2016

IV   Appendices

Sunder Kathak Katha (The wondrous tale of my Kathak): Training in Kathak and stumbling upon spiritual embodiment.

In preparation for a Kathak performance, recently I was exploring what I wished to convey in my dance and my being. The first piece I was dancing was about the perfection of life and the other was about Krishna and his mischievous nature. I felt elated when at the end of my performance a member of the audience came up to me and said that I had embodied devotion. It was the best compliment I could have received!

In essence such emotion and embodiment of dance are there in the depth of my being but they have been excavated gradually by dancing Kathak over the span of my life. My writing hopefully will convey the influence Kathak has had on the development not only of my innermost self, but how the blending of the inner propels the outer to develop in tandem. Though I write about myself it is a story of one person's influence on a landscape of the spirit of dance within and without. It is a story about taking an ordinary stone and polishing it into a precious gem. It is a story about my beloved teacher, Nilimadevi Menski, MBE and her influence on my dance.

I began my dancing at the age of eight at a primary school in Nairobi, Kenya. It was the first time I performed and the joy of dressing up was uncontainable. I had a natural ability for moving to the beats of folk music, but with this there was a sense of freedom of expressing emotions in a way that I felt quite inhibited to as a child. In dance I became someone else or something else took over.

Typically when a new community is being established, one of the first things they want is a place where they feel they belong. Community centres gave people the opportunity to celebrate through dance, music and worship to reconnect and consolidate their identity as a group. After coming to Leicester, the Navratri festival was celebrated indoors in the cold of winter. Trudging through the snow in a sari, sandals and woollies did little to affect the passion to dance. Eventually formal competitions were held at the De Montfort Hall as the 'Annual Raas Garba Competition'. I was a part of this in my teens and won a prize for 'Abhinaya' or embodied expression, which my father was very proud of.

I missed dance when I went off to become a teacher. However at the first opportunity I began to bring it into the school where I worked. I taught deaf children at a school in London at the time. I set a Garba folk dance piece on Holi, the spring festival. Teaching this to deaf children, the emphasis needed to be on the emotional content of the story. The children got it and were dancing, feeling the music in their silent worlds. It was pure joy for them to show that they, too, could have a relationship to sound and show this in a concrete way. It was brave to introduce something so alien to people's experience of dancing. My very English deaf students performed to an audience of 2,000 plus people. My headmaster, a powerful and busy man, made a point of acknowledging this spectacular achievement with joy and sincerity.

IV   Appendices

My passion for dance was rewarded when I returned to Leicester. I needed a creative outlet and a focus on more than what life offered at the time. I heard the person I came to call Didi ('older sister') later, Nilimadevi Menski, on Radio Leicester advertising classes for Kathak and was excited at the prospect of finally taking up formal training in dance. Arranging for my first class, I turned up shiny-faced and enthusiastic. I do not think Didi expected older students, however, a few of us turned up.

Those early days were a hard graft, developing the body into graceful movement. I enjoyed how this made me feel and felt elegant and graceful, though I may not have looked it. Footwork was arduous and trying to get my left foot to do what my brain wanted took patience, never mind keeping time and rhythm. Endless, 'ta thai thai tat' had purpose, but initially I could not see it. I trusted my teacher and let myself sink into the practice. Didi's foundation training was strong and in this strong frame we developed all other creativity within the reference of Jaipur Kathak. In a way Kathak was my anchor during that period of time and a strong basic training is an anchor to all that comes from it.

Opposition from my parents was subtle. They trusted my own integrity and decisions, but also held views that came from their experience of classical dance which was not favourable. It was perceived as a dance of the Moghul Courts and the morals of dancers were considered questionable. I suppose running parallel to this process was also CICD's encounter of those initial obstacles in the wider community.

One day I asked my mother to accompany me to class, where we did our normal warm-up with footwork and then danced some compositions (*todas*) about Krishna. These were my favourite and I danced them with the devotion and spiritual reverence they deserved. My mother was astounded, enthralled and relieved. From that day she embraced and accepted the fact that Kathak was a part of my life. For me it was my spiritual practice, a form connecting with more than what I was to the world. It gave me the space when I could be in complete attentive devotion to that which cannot be explained. Pandit Birju Maharaj captures something of what I am trying to say, that Kathak is one of the ways to connect with the divine. Hence he calls it 'Sadhana', meditation practice and says that when giving '*sama*' [striking a pose], let your eyes look at Krishna – this is inherent Bhakti, devotion in dance'. Footwork (*tatkar*) becomes practice of a japa, instead of 'Hare Ram Hare Krishna', we are saying 'na dhin dhin na'. Finally he says that when danced with that emotion, it connects to the divine. Ah……. the arduous footwork finally made sense!

To journey inward in a world that was externally focussed was a delicious treat and there was a knowing within me that led the way. Therefore it was not so important in what environment we danced. Yes, the space where we began our dance was cold and we did not know what our hands and feet were doing because we had no mirrors at first, but in a way we had to feel through it and remember. It was colder for my poor teacher tapping the beats for us with a wooden stick and not moving. It took a level of determination to remain focussed, and by far not everyone survived these early stages of rigorous practice. The new studio was very welcome – the mirrors were pretty misty at the end of practice sessions, as we generated so much heat!

Leicester in the early 1980s was still developing a multicultural identity and there was still a lot of racism. There was a wave of funding to support the developing strength of ethnic identity and with it came reactions of resentment from the host community. To go to extremes in claiming an identity in classical dance was going beyond what was already a sore wound in the wider community. However this was also a delicate point within the Asian community in that we were somehow drawing attention to ourselves by being so different in our clothes, food, music and dance which would only fuel the separateness.

I thwarted such stances and turned up for interviews dressed in a sari. I wore Indian outfits in office settings. I was young and confident and challenged views that were not inclusive. Through my work life I was aware of this inequality and was politically active in pursuing equality in the classroom, challenging such views on both sides, school and home, as it was hindering children's full learning potential. Once again it comes down to freedom of expression of the depth of one's being, shaped by one's cultural roots. With migration came the risk of loss of such depth. For some the fight was too big and they went into mourning the loss of their identity. Yet for the majority there was hope in raising an awareness of the richness of what was to come – a new British Asian identity!

Going back to Kathak, the most memorable of my performances are the *Triangle* performed at the Haymarket and *The Ugly Duckling* at the Phoenix. We also had the opportunity to perform to exclusive audiences of Shruti Arts, and I remember a 'Tarana' set to Ashit Desai's music. This was a complicated technical piece and a great hit with an audience that understood music and dance at depth. I thought I would retire after the *Triangle* as it met my desire to perform in a company, but Didi surprised me by offering me the lead role in *The Ugly Duckling*.

Performing the lead in *The Ugly Duckling* was the highlight of my dancing. It is a fabulous story and the children's performances were particularly endearing. It was a huge success for us as a group. It showed how versatile Kathak is and can be, without boundaries when it comes to story-telling, which is the part I love the most about Kathak. *The Ugly Duckling* offered me the scope to show the repertoire of my expressional skills in Abhinaya. It enables you to express without limitations, emotion is emotion in any language, and this became more and more evident for me as I became more familiar with the stage, realising that there was an unspoken subtle level of communication between the dancer and the audience. The essence of Kathak is very refined in this subtlety, which requires a degree of emotional depth and cognitive awareness.

We also took part in many community performances as a way of informing the

IV Appendices

community about dance. The practices were just as eventful as our performances. Our confidence developed as a group, as did our stage presence. There was cohesion and a fluidity developing and this made a great platform to form a folk dance group which Didi called 'Kalavrunda', which we took to the Edinburgh Fringe Festival. Our costumes were colourful and vibrant as were the dances. These performances were polished and professional, and they were applauded as such.

This evolving repertoire of our dance company was influenced by the variety in training we had. As a way of expanding our knowledge and creative potential in dance, Didi had exposed us to as much dance as possible. She had organised for us to experience workshops with any visiting dancer or dance group from India. With the skills and training received I put on a 'Dance Extravaganza' involving a wide range of folk dance styles. It showed how far I had travelled not only in Kathak, but also in my accomplishment in folk dances. It was a luxury to have had such experiences.

Apart from the group performances in Kathak, I undertook individual performances for school assemblies. I remember a primary school head teacher complimenting me on my way with the children, but I think it was the fluid nature of Kathak that was to be complimented, as it spoke to the children. It was while I was dancing a poem (*kavita toda*) about Krishna wanting to play with the moon. His mother Yashoda tried everything to console him and felt fed up. At this stage I asked my young audience if they could show me how to be fed up. The whole assembly of children put their hands on their heads showing me, 'fed up'! It was collaborative, engaging and emotional. That's what dance should be about. For me at that time, dance was about breaking down barriers to difference. It is about communicating the depth of our uniqueness and oneness.

Knighton Fields and the Trainee Animateur Scheme was another experience that gave something to the development of dance courses. I think it was an attempt to fit Asian dance into a Western format of teaching and learning dance. Whilst I did not partake in this, these were exploratory times.

One cannot speak about Kathak in Leicester without mentioning Guruji, Didi's Kathak teacher from Baroda. He was not the way I imagined. It was precious to benefit from his input and we performed a piece on Kathak Katha. The Guru-Shishya relationship is sacred and we could all feel this. I myself hold both Guruji and Didi in the highest esteem in my heart, for without them I would not have learnt Kathak nor expressed the beauty of movement itself.

It would be relevant to say that it has not been easy to continue with dance since leaving Leicester. Living on the edge of London for many years I mourned the loss of Kathak. Joining other Kathak groups has its challenges. Travelling distances takes its toll. Or there is a demand to start from scratch, although I was already a trained dancer under Didi, and I stuck to this stance. However, new opportunities arise every day. Performing for Didi's celebration of 30 years of dance was a pleasure and an honour. I couldn't let that pass without letting her know that all her efforts were not in vain. This performance re-awakened my desire to dance again. Since then I have performed on two other occasions. In the very writing of this piece I am reminded of what Kathak means to me, it reminds me of what was missing.

Leicester has become vibrant with the energy of dance. My dear friend Nayana still performs Kathak in many places. Perhaps the Bollywood scene has more of the stage today, but life is a constant change, nothing remains static. I guess that is the cosmic dance of Natraj (Shiva), embodied as divine dancer, indicating that we have overcome the ignorance of truth. Kathak is the truth of dance in its purest form. It cannot vanish, for it is life itself.

I think the future of South Asian dance is promising. Watching a young dancer on television, dancing for a panel awarding 'Young South Asian Dancer Awards', I felt the criteria encapsulated what was difficult to articulate in the early years of my own time as a dancer. There is a different level of integration. Long-standing dancers such as Didi herself have influenced and articulated the potential of Asian classical dance for decades. Their efforts have come to fruition because there is height and depth to Asian classical dance being recognised in Britain. It is promoting and stretching the limits of its existence, both at conscious and unconscious levels. The profile of South Asian classical dance is much more respected and honoured today, as an equal art form to classical ballet.

Gita Lakhlani
6 April 2016

IV   Appendices

Appendix 8: Reflections on the *Parampara* and *Karman* projects

Reflections on the *Parampara* project

In the mid-1990s Nilima Devi, a teacher of Indian classical dance, approached Leicester City Council's Living History Unit and asked for their help in writing a short book about the history of Indian dance and music in Leicester. A 48 page book, *Parampara* (which means 'continuing the tradition'), was published in 1996 and was one of the earliest books to look at the recent history of the South Asian communities in Leicester.

Having arrived in Leicester in 1980 Mrs Devi established the Centre for Indian Classical Dance (CICD) in 1981. She also taught in schools and neighbourhood centres as a classical dance animateur, a post created by a partnership of local agencies in 1985. Other groups, such as Shruti Arts, promoted dance and music performances in this period, while by the 1990s private dance and music schools had also become established.

By 1995 the Living History Unit had published several books about the city's history and was established as an oral history archive and local history unit at Leicester City Council. *Highfields Rangers: an oral history* (1993) was about Leicester's first African-Caribbean football team but, up to that date, the Unit had not published any other books about the city's migrant communities.

Parampara was subtitled *Thirty Years of Indian Dance and Music in Leicester* and the aim was to conduct oral history interviews that would provide memories from as far back as possible. In the event, although people had been arriving in Leicester from the Indian sub-continent since the late 1940s, the earliest memories in the book were from the mid-1960s.

The interviews were carried out in English and were recorded by Smita Vadnerkar, a dance teacher, and Colin Hyde, a local oral historian. Around twenty people were interviewed for the book and the interviewees were a mixture of teachers, performers, organisers and supporters. Although *Parampara* concentrated on dance and music, it also illustrated the changes in the more general social and cultural lives of South Asians in Leicester. Early memories are often of families and individuals going to the cinema at the weekend and spending whole afternoons watching films. As one of the contributors pointed out, 'If you are a person who is a vegetarian, a person who doesn't particularly want to go to the pub for drinking, you haven't got any social life'. So, the cinema provided one of the few places where people could meet to share their culture.

The book traces the development of events from small celebrations in peoples' homes in the early 1960s through the gradual development of dance and music events at increasingly larger sites to the use of the biggest venues in the city and the establishment of professional teaching in the 1980s and 1990s.

Up to 1996 there had been few oral histories, or social history of any sort, about any of the South Asian communities in the city or county, so *Parampara* is useful as a general history as well as a history of dance and music. Also interesting is that Nilima Devi talks about her work as a classical dance animateur, a post that was created by a partnership of the City and County Councils with East Midlands Arts and the Arts Council of Britain. This illustrates how the local authorities were responding to the increasing South Asian population in the city (the 'New Commonwealth' population of Leicester in 1961 was 4,624, while in the 1991 census over 60,000 people were identified as 'Indian'). However, it is only more recently, with the funding available from the Heritage Lottery Fund, that there have been a number of community-led heritage projects looking at the histories of people with South Asian heritage. These include a recent project about the history of the local Mela and a forthcoming project about Leicester's Diwali celebrations. As a complement to *Parampara*, in 2012 the Karman project documented the 30 year history of the CICD. Projects such as the City Museums' Kampala to Leicester and Ugandan Exodus project concentrate on the East African experience, but there are still only a few recordings with people who arrived in the 1950s and 1960s.

On a personal note, *Parampara* was the first opportunity I had had to interview people from South Asia. As well as learning about Indian dance and music, I visited some of Leicester's temples and gurdwaras (Sikh temples) for the first time and was able to get a brief idea of the histories of some of my fellow citizens whose experiences were often quite different from my own. On reflection it was an interesting and valuable experience for me.

Colin Hyde
26 January 2016

Relevant websites and references:

Leicester Mela Heritage – http://www.melaheritage.uk/
Karman – http://www.cicd.org.uk/karman_history
Kampala to Leicester – http://www.storyofleicester.info/exploreleicester/exhibitionarchive/kampalatoleicester/
Ugandan Exodus – http://www.ugex.org.uk/
1961 Census information quoted in Nash, D. & Reeder, D., *Leicester in the 20th Century* (1993), Stoud: Allan Sutton publishers, p.187.
1991 Census Information – http://cdm16445.contentdm.oclc.org/cdm/ref/collection/p16445coll2/id/4415

Reflections on the *Karman* project

I was very pleased to be invited to join the Advisory Board for the *Karman* project. I had worked with Nilima in the Arts Advisory section at Leicester City Council when the

IV Appendices

Living History Unit was established there in 1992, and learned something about Asian dance through that contact and the *Parampara* book compiled by my colleagues to mark 30 years of Asian dance in Leicester. After leaving the City Council in 2001 I helped to set up the East Midlands Oral History Archive at the University of Leicester, so felt I could bring both my oral history experience and local historical knowledge to the project.

The oral histories collected by the project volunteers were central to the story of CICD itself, often providing information that was simply not available elsewhere. They were still more interesting to me in terms of what dancing meant to the participants and what they learned about themselves in the process, which was not a dimension I had previously considered. 'Dance makes me feel I am part of this world', one of them said: 'like I can say what I want to say without fear of being different and it fundamentally allows me to be me, free and uninhibited'. Another simply wanted to 'have fun and learn an art form. However, with the spiritual component of Kathak I became aware of my own spirituality and have developed it further... These were my first foundations of my spiritual identity'.

Oral histories are often of great value in illuminating this kind of personal experience, and offering unexpected insights. I had not realised, for instance, that the parents of some students – or in one instance her in-laws – were opposed to them learning classical dance: and then her own family was 'not very happy' when she encouraged her daughter to learn in turn. It 'was associated in their minds with popular films', another explained, and she 'had to hide her dance classes from her father, telling him that she was visiting a friend's house'.

My knowledge of the history of migration to Leicester did prove useful in placing it in context from the 19th century onwards, but I learnt much more in other respects than I contributed. As the various strands of the project came together for the book and exhibition, I realised how little I knew of the wider history of Asian dance, globally or nationally, and its cultural, artistic and historical significance in Britain: of its development from the 'colourful stranger' of the 1920s to the post-World War II movement to present Indian culture to wider audiences, for instance, as well as the 30 years of CICD itself. Nor had I given much thought to how Asian dance may develop in the future until reading the final section of the *Karman* book. The consensus from those involved is that the future is bright: that for many people in Britain with Asian roots it has become an integral part of daily life, 'hybridity in action', which seems to promise 'a peaceful and safe journey into the future'. It is one that I will continue to watch with interest.

Cynthia Brown
22 August 2015

Appendix 9: The history of the Indian classical dance in Leicester (Extracts from the *Leicester Mercury*)

1

Saturday, September 12, 1981

Telling stories by dancing

The story-telling Kathak style of Northern Indian classical dance was demonstrated last night by the Moat Community College-based Highfields Kathak Group. The programme was split between a technical, or pure dance part, and the telling of stories about Rama, Sita, and Lord Krishna, through facial expressions, gestures and symbolic postures.

Solo dancer was Mrs Nilima Devi, who was born in Baroda, Gujarat. She was one of the most promising dancers in the region before she moved to West Germany in 1977 and to Leicester last year. Mrs Devi has established an Institute of Indian Classical Dance in the city to develop knowledge and interest in classical and medieval Indian art. She was accompanied yesterday by two professional musicians from London, Mr Ismail Sheikh on table and Mr Ramprasad Joshi on harmonium.

Caption: The audience watching Nilima Devi, the solo dancer, performing during the demonstration of Northern Indian classical dancing presented by the Highfields Kathak Group.

2

Friday, March 12, 1982

Ethnic Arts Grants 'Should be Tripled'

Ethnic arts in Leicester and the East Midlands should be given three times as much cash to develop fully, say authors of a report after a long-term survey.

This would not be positive discrimination, but merely "fair shares for all," says East Midlands Arts Association director Mr Anthony Everitt.

The association now devotes just over £10,000 a year towards ethnic art groups and individuals. That is slightly less than two per cent of total grants of £555,650. Over the next three years they want to increase the proportion to six per cent of their grants budget. Their report – more than two years in the compiling – was launched at Moat Community College, Sparkenhoe Street, Leicester.

Mr Everitt agreed that the association were making up for past omissions in neglecting the important contribution that ethnic art could make to the cultural wealth of the region. He urged ethnic art experts, both from minority white and black communities, to work with the association in developing the potential. "We desperately need their expertise to help us assess the importance and significance of work being done," he said. He offered the carrot of increased Government aid via the Arts Council if a strong case could be prepared.

3

Thursday, April 19, 1984

Darting steps that bring a faith alive
Ancient dance tells a story
By Ather Mirza

Strutting like a peacock, darting her eyes with the menacing of a snake-Nilima Devi holds her audience captive.

Every mesmerising movement is timed to perfection, turned to the strains of the sitar and harmonium, and the regular beat of the table. Ankle-bells jangle with each step as another story is told by Kathak, an ancient North India classical dance. A rich repertoire of gestures and expressions convey symbols that, for many Indians, express their faith. Kathak is story-telling through dance. The name derives from the Sanskrit words for 'story' and 'making' and dances often relate religious fables or epic tales of heroism in Indian mythology.

International Kathak dancer, Nilima Devi, who lives in Leicester, is one of the most skilled exponents of this art. Grace characterises every finely-wrought movement and delicate gesture. "As a devout Hindu, I feel Kathak is part of my faith. I do not get to pray but when I dance it is my dedication to God, my own form of worship" said 30-year-old Mrs Devi, who has been in Leicester for three years. "When I began learning Kathak in India at the age of six, the dance gave me a spiritual feeling and much pleasure and peace. After marriage, I became keen to teach my culture through dance," she added.

Ballet is perhaps the nearest European equivalent to Kathak, but people still have many misconceptions about one of India's most ancient dances. "Kathak was used to teach people morality. Hindu scriptures are in Sanskrit, so singing, hand movements and mime developed in the temples to explain stories.

Romantic

"After the Muslim invasion of India, Kathak developed as a romantic form and court-dancing was patronised." Children from four-years-old are encouraged to learn Kathak at Mrs Devi's home, the Institute of Classical Indian Dance, Churchill Street, Leicester.

About 20 girls regularly attend once a week to learn the art from Mrs Devi, who has a master's degree in Kathak. "It takes 10 years to get a complete sense of rhythm and perfect coordination."

Gujarat-born Mrs Devi, whose mother tongue is Marathi, prefaces each of her public demonstrations with an explanation of the intricate movements, and the story her dance is about to relate. Mrs Devi, who has two children, is keen for more people of all backgrounds to learn Kathak. She also holds lessons at Moat Community College, Maidstone Road, Leicester and in Nottingham.

4

Tuesday, September 4, 1984

Dance studio opened

A new studio at the city's Institute of Classical Indian Dance, Churchill Street, was officially opened by the Lord Mayor and Lady Mayoress, Mr Michael Cufflin and his wife, Susan. After cutting the tape they joined guests inside the £8,000 extension for a performance given by some of the school's young pupils. The institute, known as Nilmani Kathak Kendra (Black Bead Kathak Centre) was started by its dance teacher, Mrs Nilima Devi, in 1981.

Kathak is a form of story-telling through dance, originally performed inside Hindu temples. Mrs Devi began her formal training in the technique at 13, and obtained a master's degree in 1976. She came to England four years later to establish the institute, which occupies two converted terraced houses. The aims of the institute are to foster interest in Indian art and dance, offering a six year diploma course. At present there are 13 pupils. But the new facilities will help the dance school to expand.

5

Friday, October 17, 1986

Indian dance displays sparkle

A feast for the eyes is the best way to describe the first night of the Dance Now Festival at the Haymarket Studio. In this, the Indian Dance night, the performance was superbly choreographed and the creative atmosphere was enhanced by the beautiful clothes. Brought to the Studio by Leicester City Council Community Arts and the theatre's Art Development team, the evening began a three night festival with the first half of each show devoted to local groups. Professional groups from around the country take the floor in the second half.

IV   Appendices

Portrayed

Dance animators Nilima Devi and Piali Ray, who both work for East Midlands Arts, together with their students, showed the wealth of local talent, and professional couple Pushkala Gopal and Unnikrishnan gave a sparkling display of dance and mime. The evening was made even more enjoyable as simple descriptions were given before each dance so the stories portrayed could be easily understood. Tonight the Studio offers Polish dancing, with Afro-Caribbean music on Saturday. Both promise to be spectacular.

— Heather Clarke

Caption: Unni Krishnan (right), of the Academy of Indian Dance, puts dancers from Abbey Primary School and Leicester Polytechnic through their paces at an Indian dance workshop, part of the multi-cultural dance festival at the Haymarket Theatre.

6

Friday, March 31, 1989

Multi-cultural evening in Leicester

Westcotes Library in Leicester celebrated its centenary this month with a multi-cultural evening. Based at Narborough Road, Leicester which is a multi-racial area, part of the celebration, included a Ukrainian Dance Group, Women's Morris Dancers, Asian Dance and much more. Pictured is Nayana Whittaker performing a graceful dance from the Rajasthan area of India, at the special evening on 22 March.

7

Tuesday, March 24, 1992

Dance showcase held in city
Music and Art Blended at Gallery
By Deedar Bahra and Vasant Kalyani

City Gallery in Granby Street recently echoed with the sound of Eastern music. The evening began with a classical dance followed by Raas and Garba, and a traditional Matka Dance portraying the joy of fetching water was well received by the audience. Youngsters dressed in traditional costume presented the variety performance that enthralled the guests.

The whole event was organized by City Gallery and Nilima Devi, Asian Dance Development Officer with Leicester City Council to coincide with the Crossing Black Waters exhibition. Local Indian Dance groups from Jain Samaj Group, Shree Sanatan Centre, Nupur Arts presented a wide range of talents. Nilima Devi, the organizer said:

"All the young people were truly appreciated for their talents and we hope this will be an ongoing event at the City Gallery."

8

Thursday, September 3, 1992

Prithi Dances to Success

A Leicester woman has passed an A-level course in South Asian Dance, at the Charles Keene College.

Ms Prithi Raithatha, pictured above, undertook the two-year course in 1990. One of only three students, she soon found herself alone as the other two decided to leave the course midway. The condensed course took Prithi through an arduous course of Kathak, Bharat Natya Ballet as well as Contemporary dancing under the guidance of some of the best tutors including Kumar Saswat, Nilima Devi, Pandit Sundarlal Gangani, as well as Dean Macqueen and Liz Valantine. Prithi said of her success: "A lot of hard work went into preparing for the course because it was the first of its kind. I am hoping to enroll on the BA Degree course at the De Montfort University. I just want to be a student for the rest of my life."

9

Wednesday, March 3, 1993

Proving Helping Hands around the World
By Nirmala Bhojani

An evening of international entertainment, food and fund-raising was organised by the Leicester Christian Fellowship to raise money for the charity Help International, at Hessed House, Frog Island, Leicester. Mr Daljinder Padam of the Leicester Christian Fellowship welcomed the Lord Mayor Councillor Bob Wigglesworth and the Lady Mayoress Mrs Colleen Wigglesworth and the guests. He said: "We hope to bring out the best of all the cultures and to promote an awareness of the different cultures that exist here." He also introduced Mr S Ogrodzinski, Director of Help International.

Medical projects

Mr Ogrodzinski spoke about the work of the charity, based in Wolvey, Leicestershire, which operated as 'Help Africa' in 1985 in response to a local medical need in Zambia. It then extended its work to other parts of Africa – Zimbabwe, Namibia, Mozambique and Uganda, initiating medical projects, irrigation schemes and education centres to be set up. The charity formed two more branches 'Help Asia' and 'Help Europe' setting up

IV   Appendices

various projects all over these continents. Their success soon resulted in the three branches joining together to form 'Help International'.

The entertainment programme included music and dances from China, Malaysia, India, England and Poland, England and Poland. Each act was followed by an auction of donated items to raise funds for 'Help International'. RimZim, a classical Indian Kathak dance by Shivani Watt and Nimisha Patel gave the audience a glimpse of the exotic Indian subcontinent. The auction conducted by Mr Stuart Pettifer raised £708. Mrs Jatinder Sembi introduced each act and helped in organising the displays of musical instruments, jewellery and traditional handicrafts from China, India, Australasia, America, Africa, Poland and England.

Caption:
  Above: Indian Kathak dance by Shivani Watt ad Nimisha Patel.
  Right: Malaysian Ribbon Dance by children of Leicester Malaysian Society.

10

Monday, August 30, 1993

Spirited Youth Group in City Show
Dancer joins youth group

City dancer, Shivani Satya, is to help a national youth company stage its latest production in Leicester. The Kathak dancer trained by city teacher, Nilima Devi, will take part in Yuva (youth), a production by the Youth Dance Company of Aditi, the national organisation for South Asian Dance. Shivani trained under Nilima Devi, for six years and has performed across the Midlands, in London and at the Edinburgh fringe festival. For its new production, the Yuva Dance Company, which is this year based in Leicester, has chosen two new works called 'Spirited Youth' and 'In the Mix'. The works will be premiered at Moat Community College on September 11 at 7.30 pm and will then tour nationally'.

Caption
  SHIVANI: Set to perform in premiere of Aditi youth group show.

11

Thursday, March 24, 1994

Song and Dance Marks Muslim Festival
By Vasant Kalyani

Leicester Asian Youth Association on Evington Valley Road, Leicester, celebrated the

IV Appendices

Muslim festival of Eid-Ul-Fitr with a variety of entertainment. Students from Sangeet Sabha of the Leicestershire School of Arts performed excellently on sitar and tabla. Members of the Asian Youth Group at Woodgate Resource Centre, trained and choreographed by Vaidehi Pancholi, presented Indian folk dances. And Institute of Indian Dance trainees performed beautiful classical Kathak dances. Musical entertainment was provided by Shabab from Birmingham. Singers Anjuman, Iqbal Khan and Ansar Khalid performed popular film songs and qawalis. LAYA centre manager, Mr Mohammed Nasim, said: "On this day we wish all our brothers and sisters a very happy and prosperous Eid."

Caption:
Happy Time: Left, traditional folk dancers perform at LAYA's spectacular Eid celebrations. Above, children are enthralled by the entertainment provided.

12

Friday, May 6, 1994

Focus on Traditional Activities
Multi-cultural event is held at local centre

Lansdowne Neighbourhood Centre on Knighton Lane held its first multi-cultural evening of activities recently.

Mehndi (hand painting), garland making, origami and Asian make-up were some the attractions at the event. Visitors were treated to a display of traditional dance. Ten-year-old Reena Patel performed an item from Indian film. Nayana Whittaker presented a traditional Rajasthani folk dance. Members of the audience also had the chance to learn about traditional Indian dress. A spokesperson said the centre hoped to hold a similar event later in the year.

Caption:
Heritage: Activities at a special event at Lansdowne Neighbourhood centre included traditional make-up, Rajasthani dance and origami.

13

Wednesday, June 15, 1994

Students Perform Song and Dance
Popular festival held
By Ian Whittaker

As part of the Leicestershire Schools Festival at the Haymarket Theatre in Leicester

IV   Appendices

Sangeet Sabha held an evening of music and dance. Packed audiences at the two performances were entertained by a programme of skilled vocal recitals, sitar and tabla ensembles and intricate Kathak dance. Sangeet Sabha chairman County Councillor Hasmukh Jobanputra thanked teachers, pupils and Haymarket staff for all their hard work in preparing the successful performances. Sangeet Sabha students will also be performing for the American Dream production at the Haymarket Theatre. Sangeet Sabha is the Leicestershire Arts in Education Asian performance group.

Caption:
   Presentations: Students of Sangeet Sabha performing at the schools festival held recently at the Haymarket Theatre in Leicester.

14

Friday, June 24, 1994

North American Indian Customs Inspire Students' Production
By Ian Whittaker

Leicestershire Schools South Asian Dance Scheme students opened the spectacular Stars and Stripes production held recently. The theme of the performance was taken from the rituals and customs of North American Indians. Aspects of daily life such as canoeing, farming, hunting and fishing, as well as celebrations and mourning were conveyed through mime and acting. Dancers portrayed how the tranquillity of village life was frequently interrupted by periods of warfare and the regrouping of tribal alliances. The item, choreographed by Nilima Devi, was set to traditional North American Indian music. Stars and stripes was the final production in a two-week-festival by Leicestershire schools.

Caption:
   Ready for action: A battle scene from the Haymarket Theatre's recent Stars and Stripes production performed by students of Leicestershire Schools South Asian Dance Scheme.

15

Wednesday, August 24, 1994

Youngsters Explore the Role of Classical Dance
Workshops in dance

Workshops in classical dance were held at Knighton Fields Centre. Students explored different dance forms to see how they can be used to influence modern Asian creative dance. Bisakha Sarakar, a renowned dance artist based in the United Kingdom gave a workshop in creative Indian dance based on the philosophy of Uday Shankar. The master classes are part of a summer school of Indian dance organised by the Arts Advisory Section of Leicester City Council, Leicestershire Arts and Nilima Devi.

Caption: Exploration: Young dancers from across the county took part in dance workshops organised to explore the use of Indian classical dance on the contemporary stage in Britain.

16

Friday, December 2, 1994

Round-Up of Community Arts and Entertainments Events
Classical show staged
By Vasant Kalyani

A showcase of Indian music and dance was recently presented by the Friends of Sangeet Sabha – Leicestershire Arts. The evening's entertainment, co-sponsored by the Arpan Insurance Agency and Midland Bank, attracted a large crowd. This was the second such annual event. It included classical music featuring sitar and tabla and classical Kathak dancing. Hasmukh Jobanputra, Sangeet Sabha chairman, said: "This programme combines skilled recitals by singers and sitar and tabla play with intricate performances of Kathak dance. All the young performers study their chosen discipline as part of the Leicestershire Arts training programme. Sangeet Sabha has built a national reputation for their outstanding performances."

Sangeet Sabha has recently bought more instruments so more students will benefit from use of the normally expensive equipment. The evening began with a candle dance followed by singing and sitar and tabla playing. Bhavini Gohil gave a polished presentation as did all the performers. The students were taught by Gurmeet Singh Virdee, Tirlok Singh, Ramnik Varu, Surinder Singh Sondh and Nilima Devi.

Caption:
   Music: A sitar ensemble, part of the Sangeet Sabra event held at Rushey Mead Secondary.

17

Tuesday, January 30, 1996

Dancers win finals spot

An Asian dance group based in Leicester has won through to the regional finals of a national festival of dance.

IV   Appendices

Kalavrund, a group taught by Nayana Whittaker, was picked from more than 250 youth dance groups across the country to perform in one of the 10 regional finals of the UK BT Festival of Dance. The group will be performing a traditional Indian stick dance called Raas. The dance style is normally performed during the Indian festival of Navratri. The place has been set to modern romantic Bollywood film song instead of the more traditional folk dance music. Anyone interested in learning Indian folk can contact Mrs Whittaker through the Shree Sanatan Community Project on 0116 266 6156. Classes run on Tuesday and Wednesday evenings from 6pm until 9pm at the Belgrave Neighbourhood Centre.

Caption

Success: All set for the UK BT Festival of Dance regional finals are, back row, from left: Bhavika Mistry, 17, Reeva Mistry, 14, Sheetal Kavia, 15, Rakhee Thaker, 15, Bhavini Gohil, 15 and Rina Babla, 13. Front row: Vibhuti Chahan, 14, Sangita Mistry, 13, Sujata Parmar, 18, Jeamini Mistry, 15, and Vanisha Mistry, 12.

18

Friday, February 16, 1996

Dancers step forward

A Leicester dance group is performing French opera in the city. The Shree Sanatan Centre's dance group (pictured) directed by Nayana Whittaker have been invited to take part in the Ashleyan Opera presentation of the Clement Philibert Leo Delibes Opera's Lakme. The show is currently being staged at the Little Theatre in Dover Street. Telephone the theatre on Leicester 2551 302 for further information.

19

Wednesday, My 15, 1996

Dance Mission to Ireland is a Success
City team return from cultural mission to the Irish Republic
By Ian Whittaker

Members of a Leicester dance group have returned after performing at the prestigious Cork International Choral Festival in Southern Ireland. The dedicated team of dancers from the Shree Sanatan Asian Dance Group were successful in reaching the estimated total cost of £2,000 through various fund-raising efforts held in the city. The Belgrave dancers were chosen by organisers of the festival from a total of 140 invitations that were sent out.

IV   Appendices

The score of young girls performed traditional Indian folk dancing at the gala concerts during the major four-day festival in front of audiences exceeding 1,000 people a night. During their stay in Ireland the group entertained in schools and also gave public performances. The team, dressed in glittering costumes, created great impact among all their public audiences and provided a striking visual contrast to the more serious dimension of the festival. Their public performances helped to increase the awareness of the major festival taking place in Cork.

Miss Bavika Mistry, a dancer in the team, said: "This was a new experience for me. I've never done anything like this before. Like all the members of the dance team I was very excited about performing on stage. I felt lucky that I was included in the trip. The training and performing in Leicester and at the festival in Cork was very hard work, but it was all great fun." Teacher Ms Nayana Whittaker led the team.

Caption:
   Cultural mission: Members of the Shree Sanatan Asian Dance group at the festival in Cork; Below: Shoppers watch a performance at a shopping centre in the Irish city.

20

Thursday, February 12, 1998

Classical show for young

Talented young students of Indian classical dance and music feature their creative work in the Vividh showcase at Phoenix Theatre, Leicester, on Sunday, March 21. This highly popular annual showcase features students from Sangeet Sabha, the established Indian dance and music group of Leicester and Leicestershire Arts in Education. The students have learned their craft from dedicated teachers including Gurmeet Singh Virdee (tabla), Ramnik Varu (vocal), Tirlok Singh (sitar) and Nilima Devi (Kathak dance). While the first half concentrates on North Indian classical music and Kathak by students of Sangeet Sabha, the second half features the cultural heritage of Gujarat.

Here, the performances involve a combination of prachin (traditional) and arvachin (contemporary) garba dance forms by South Asian community dance groups in Leicester. Nilima Devi, one of the teachers responsible for bringing out the best in her students, said: "We have selected the best young talent who are trained in our classical traditions at schools and on Saturday mornings in North Indian classical dance and music. We also have students trained at various community centres. We have started to give a theme to the community showcase. Last year it was the folk dance of India. This year the theme is the cultural heritage of the Gujarat." For further information, contact the Phoenix Theatre box office on Leicester 255 4854.

Caption:

IV   Appendices

Notes: The Vividh showcase at Phoenix Theatre, in Leicester, will highlight the talents of young students.

21

Thursday, October 22, 1998

Youngsters shine

City youngsters from Sandfield Close Primary School, Rushey Mead, Leicester, and Shree Sanatan Community Project put on a spectacular concert of music, dance and drama to celebrate Diwali. Proud parents, family and friends were entertained by Year Four and Five pupils wearing bright and colourful Indian costumes. Youngsters learning classical music at the school displayed their skills on sitar, harmonium and tabla. Some recited poetry and talked on the significance of Diwali while others performed a play. Girls under the tuition of dance lecturers and performers Mrs Nilima Devi and Mrs Nayana Whittaker put on a performance of both classical and contemporary dance. Parents witnessed complicated drama sequences performed with relative ease and assurance by the children. Headmistress Mrs Janet McClaran said: "Programmes like this teach children to live with each other and give them a greater understanding of other faiths, cultures and religions."

Caption: Young talent: Pupils who took part in a spectacular Diwali concert included (back row, left to right) Gurpreet Kaur Jutla, Radhika Kukadia and Misha Thakrar and (front row, left to right) Jaiminee Mistry, Ashka Shah and Garima Rathod.

22

Thursday, June 19, 2003

Thinks... I Really Feel Like Dancing

East meets West in Nilima Devi's new show at the Phoenix. Jane Ford dips into the cultural melting pot.

It may be a fuddy-duddy point of view, but there's something to be said for tradition. After all who wants to lose sight of their cultural roots and heritage? Especially if that includes beautiful dance and music. Not Indian choreographer Nilima Devi, who has a burning passion for classical Kathak dance. But tradition is a guide not a jailer. And, what is more, she hasn't let that stop her delving into a less customary dance form. In her latest spectacular production, Nilima returns to an old favourite. Irish dance, which she drew on in last year's Flaming Feet.

This time around, the fancy footwork of the folk from across the waters is combined with contemporary and classical Kathak repertoires to tell the story of how migration from India to the West has influenced South Asian classical artists. It looks at the integration of rhythm, dance and music to create a contemporary movement vocabulary and unique choreography. Images is the result of Nilima's experimentation and collaborative combination which will be accompanied by Indian classical musicians as well as Western musicians – including the use of harp and jazz music – and digital video. By switching melodious and rhythmic structures, Nilima Devi reveals the 'Images' of Kathak which define and represent its stylistic uniqueness.

Information

Images will be performed at Phoenix Arts on Thursday, July 3, at 8 pm. Tickets cost £8, £6 for concessions, and are available from the box office on 0116 255 4854.

23

Tuesday, September 2, 2003

Nilima fuses Kathak and Irish traditions

TA, THAI, THAI, TA might be the traditional beats to Kathak dancing but Leicester's Nilima Devi has put her own spin on things by adding Blarney influences to her cultural dancing pot. Internationally acclaimed north Indian classical dancer, Nilima has been instrumental in bringing Kathak to the forefront of dance in Leiester.

Not scared to experiment and fuse, her production of Flaming Feet, was like a Guinness with a curry top – a cohesion of two different dance forms and traditions of music, combining the rhythms and disciplines of Indian classical Kathak with traditional Irish performance. Inspired by Michael Flatley productions of River Dance and Lord of the Dance, Devi's work relies on the skills of only a handful of dancers. What Devi managed to achieve with Flaming Feet was a unity between the West and the East to bring something classically unique, and an inspiration to young children throughout Leicester.

Music Producer Richi Rich has worked with Misteeq, Craig David and Jay Sean and bought together a host of Punjabi and R & B remixes, taking the mainstream and Asian music charts by storm. He said: "It's a great moment for Asians across the world. Although I don't know much about the history, I know that it's a prestigious event for Asians. It's an overwhelming feeling for Indians living in India. I usually spend the day with the family as I know this day is important to them."

Singing sensation Apache Indian, who had hot hits such as Chakde, Arranged Marriage and Boom Shaka Lak, said: "I would like to wish everyone a happy independence day. I hope that the world can finally see what Indians at home and abroad have to offer." "I think we need to see more going back to our mother country, to the people that matter!

IV   Appendices

There is plenty to celebrate but still lots to do!"

The link between Bombay Dreams and India is unquestionable, Raj Ghatak, who has been playing the role of Sweety for the past year, feels proud as British Asian to represent India. "I think it's a momentous occasions to the efforts of Mahatama Gandhi and to all the other Indians that struggled. I feel very proud as a British Asian to be associated with the efforts of such greatness. From a musical viewpoint I think of the National Anthem and envisage the Indian Flag."

24

Wednesday, November 19, 2003

Asian events will go on the record
Unique: New archive celebrates South Asian arts and culture
By Ciaran Fagan, social affairs correspondent

A unique archive celebrating the richness of South Asian arts is set to be based in Leicester.

The archive, to be held at the University of Leicester, will be made up of books, poetry and photographic records of major performances in the city and further afield. The South Asian Diaspora Literature and Arts Archive (SADLAA) will form the basis of a host of public events. Although still in its early stages, the archive includes collections of creative literature and recordings of visual arts, theatre and performing arts. It will also highlight a mixture of published written works.

Dr Anshuman Mondal, of the university's department of English, said: "This is not going to be an archive that gathers dust. Exhibitions and other events will bring this material out to the people of Leicester and beyond." Leicester City Council believes the presence of the archive at the university will highlight the city's standing as one of the most diverse and harmonious cities in the country. Richard Watson, director of cultural services at Leicester City Council, said: "This initiative will provide a unique and invaluable record of the culture and heritage of the South Asian community in Leicester."

Nilima Devi, founder of the Institute of Indian Classical Dance, in Churchill Street, Highfields, welcomed the move. She said: "It's very important to create an archive of everything that is happening. We live in a society where understanding for each other's cultures is essential. It will also help young people learn about their roots." The archive will be launched in the city today by Lord Bhikhu Parekh, chair of the Commission on the Future of Multi-Ethnic Britain. Other speakers at the launch, at the New Walk Museum at 6pm, will include renowned musician Baluji and writer and academic Avtar Brah.

25

Tuesday, March 2, 2004

Tracing South Asian stars in the limelight 40 years ago

Do you recognise this singer? She was part of the arts scene in Leicester in the 1960s, says Dev Diwana, who is compiling a history of the contribution made to the city's arts by South Asian performers in the period from 1960 to 1999.

As impresario for hundreds of shows, Mr Diwana remembers many of the performers for whom he provided a stage – at the Corn Exchange Hall in Market Place, the Edward Wood Hall in London Road, the YMCA Hall in Granby Street, Wesley Hall in Hartington Road, the Top Rank Suite at the Haymarket and the old Sangham Cinema in Belgrave Gate. Mr Diwana and his friends in the Asian Arts Association remember stick dancers Sudha Shah, Prabhavati, Raksha Modi, Neena, Ayana, Hemlata, Shushi, Kirit and Lata. Garba dancers, whose names they remember, include H Joshi, Meena, Hansa, Lalita, Ranjan Bhatt, Harshilla, Vasant Patel, Usha, Bahwsar and Pushpa Patel. From the late 1960s, they remember Indian classical dancers Kumari Hansa, Naina Whittaker and Nilima Devi, singers Saroj Patel and Ayoub Vorha, and ghazal singer Mr A Din. Groups included Milan Music Group and the Sangham Music and Art Society.

The Asian Arts Association wants to contact anyone who remembers seeing any of these or the many others who Mr Diwana remembers – or people who performed with them. The association hopes to compile a booklet and create a video documentary chronicling those happy days. Mr Diwana, who went on from being a dancer to a playwright, and film-maker in Mumbai (Bombay) and here in Leicestershire, remembers running from one cinema to another on a Saturday morning to see as many films as possible. "It's a shame," he says "that these days we do not have anything like Sangham Arts, which used to encourage arts from all South Asian traditions." Anyone able to help Mr Diwana – perhaps by mentioning this article to older members of the community who might not know English well – should ring him on 0116 271 2749.

26

Wednesday December 19, 2012

Community heroes are inspirational

Congratulations to all the people from Leicestershire and Rutland who have received awards in the New Year's Honours. The national headlines today will be dominated by star names who have already been showered with praise in their illustrious careers. That is not meant to begrudge them the honours now conferred on them. They are worthy

IV Appendices

recipients.

However, it is particularly pleasing to see the honours system used to recognize people whose hard work and commitment contributes so much to the community, but whose efforts often go unsung.

Janet Gaskell, for instance, has played an important role over the course of many years in Leicester's Caribbean Carnival, helping to make it an annual fixture in Leicester. We are delighted that she has been made an MBE. It is fascinating to see she was inspired by seeing a festival in Antigua in 1984 where she was captivated by the "expression of joy and freedom and music and colour". That quote sums up what the parade brings to Leicester each summer.

Recognition

Likewise, it is good to see the recognition given to all the other individuals whose dedication to their communities has played an instrumental role across a diverse range of activities, from the Centre for Indian Classical Dance, in Leicester, to a local youth club in the village of Great Oxendon, near Market Harborough.

The New Year's Honours system was once in danger of becoming old-fashioned and outdated; no more than a series of gongs for Whitehall civil servants and the like. However, over the past few years it has seen the inclusion of individuals for their work in communities up and down Britain and this has given it a new lease of life.

It now seems more relevant to the lives of normal people and something which gives us all something to celebrate. The example set by those in today's list will also help to inspire the community champions of the future to come forward and continue the sort of work that makes such a difference to the lives of so many people.

(Reproduced with the permission of the Leicester Mercury)

Appendix 10: Ethnicity and Religion in the UK and Leicester [Survey of Leicester, 1983]

Table 1 Ethnic origin

Ethnic origin	Number	%
White	214,355	74.9
Asian	63,186	22.1
West Indian	5,084	1.8
Chinese	552	0.2
Mixed	1,387	0.5
Other	1,444	0.5
Not stated	12	0.0
Total	286,020	100

Table 2 Religion by ethnic origin

Religion	Ethnic origin								Total	
	White		Asian		West Indian		Other			
	Number	%	Number	%	Number	%	Number	%	Number	%
Christian	182,226	85.0	1,004	1.6	3,973	78.1	1,720	50.7	188,923	66.1
Hindu	320	0.1	39,228	62.1	44	0.9	151	4.5	39,743	13.9
Sikh	151	0.1	10,576	16.7	6	0.1	75	2.2	10,808	3.8
Muslim	332	0.2	11,614	18.4	107	2.1	383	11.3	12,436	4.3
None	28,784	13.4	482	0.8	703	13.8	721	21.2	30,690	10.7
Other	1,751	0.8	276	0.4	232	4.6	283	8.3	2,542	0.9
Not stated	791	0.4	6	—	19	0.4	62	1.8	878	0.3
Total	214,355	100	63,186	100	5,084	100	3,395	100	286,020	100

IV Appendices

Table 3 Ethnic origin by ward

Ward	Ethnic origin											Total population	
	White		Asian		West Indian		Other		Not stated			
	Number	%	Number	%	Number	%	Number	%	Number	%	Number	%
Abbey	4,683	49.0	4,803	50.2	50	0.5	24	0.3	—	—	9,560	100
Aylestone	10,394	96.0	180	1.7	175	1.6	81	0.7	—	—	10,830	100
Beaumont Leys	10,550	84.7	1,289	10.3	324	2.6	293	2.4	—	—	12,456	100
Belgrave	6,004	47.1	6,521	51.2	180	1.4	31	0.2	—	—	12,736	100
Castle	8,426	82.8	1,140	11.2	199	2.0	411	4.0	6	0.1	10,182	100
Charnwood	5,306	43.8	6,365	52.5	330	2.7	112	0.9	—	—	12,113	100
Coleman	6,633	78.9	1,351	16.1	212	2.5	212	2.5	—	—	8,408	100
Crown Hills	3,357	34.2	6,109	62.2	243	2.5	81	0.8	25	0.3	9,815	100
East Knighton	8,862	95.2	386	4.1	19	0.2	38	0.4	—	—	9,305	100
Evington	8,519	95.5	293	3.3	37	0.4	75	0.8	—	—	8,924	100
Eyres Monsell	10,170	97.7	25	0.2	118	1.1	100	1.0	—	—	10,413	100
Humberstone	10,177	97.0	268	2.6	25	0.2	24	0.2	—	—	10,494	100
Latimer	2,635	35.7	4,689	63.5	44	0.6	18	0.2	—	—	7,386	100
Mowmacre	8,756	95.3	156	2.2	38	0.5	137	1.9	—	—	7,087	100
New Parks	11,403	98.9	25	0.2	38	0.3	62	0.5	—	—	11,528	100
North Braunstone	8,774	98.3	38	0.4	44	0.5	62	0.7	6	0.1	8,924	100
Rowley Fields	7,810	87.0	984	11.0	37	0.4	137	1.5	6	0.1	8,974	100
Rushey Mead	5,474	43.5	6,776	53.9	218	1.7	106	0.8	6	—	12,580	100
Saffron	10,464	97.1	162	1.5	49	0.5	99	0.9	—	—	10,774	100
St. Augustines	8,508	89.4	896	9.4	31	0.3	81	0.9	—	—	9,516	100
Spinney Hill	2,329	22.8	7,312	70.9	573	5.6	87	0.8	6	0.1	10,307	100
Stoneygate	5,523	64.7	2,678	31.4	187	2.2	150	1.8	—	—	8,538	100
Thurncourt	10,568	96.1	262	2.4	106	1.0	62	0.6	—	—	10,998	100
Westcotes	7,728	72.0	2,573	24.0	187	1.7	243	2.3	—	—	10,731	100
Western Park	10,768	92.3	623	5.3	162	1.4	112	1.0	—	—	11,665	100
West Humberstone	6,714	75.1	1,943	21.7	162	1.8	118	1.3	6	0.1	8,943	100
West Knighton	8,817	90.5	654	6.7	150	1.5	125	1.3	—	—	9,746	100
Wycliffe	5,337	49.1	4,154	38.2	1,108	10.2	275	2.5	—	—	10,874	100
Total	212,689	74.9	62,655	22.1	5,046	1.8	3,356	1.2	61	—	283,807	100

IV Appendices

Table 4 Place of birth

Place of birth	Number	%	Total from 1981 Census	
			Number	%
England, Scotland and Wales	226,600	79.2	222,388	80.5
Northern Ireland	1,600	0.6	1,299	0.5
Irish Republic	3,000	1.0	3,886	1.4
Other European Country	3,023	1.1	3,582	1.3
West Indies/Guyana	2,530	0.9	2,551	0.9
India	20,706	7.2	18,235	6.6
Pakistan	1,086	0.4	911	0.4
Bangladesh	616	0.2	394	0.1
Kenya	9,810	3.4	8,052	2.9
Uganda	6,678	2.3	5,604	2.0
Malawi	2,649	0.9	2,323	0.8
Tanzania	2,730	1.0	2,224	0.8
Zambia	610	0.2	419	0.2
Other Africa	860	0.3	463	0.2
Other	3,283	1.2	3,914	1.4
Not stated	239	0.1	—	—
Total	286,020	100	276,245	100

IV Appendices

Table 5 First language spoken by religion

First language	Religion										Total	
	Christian		Hindu		Sikh		Muslim		None or other			
	Number	%	Number	%	Number	%	Number	%	Number	%	Number	%
English	183,626	97.2	835	2.1	546	5.1	709	5.7	31,539	92.5	217,255	76.0
Other European languages	2,078	1.1	163	0.4	—	—	6	0.1	232	0.7	2,479	0.9
Gujarati	226	0.1	36,084	90.8	326	3.0	5,178	41.6	408	1.2	42,222	14.8
Punjabi	56	—	948	2.4	9,572	88.6	716	5.8	163	0.5	11,455	4.0
Kutchi	88	—	13	—	—	—	2,930	23.6	26	0.1	3,057	1.0
Bengali	25	—	50	0.1	—	—	792	6.4	81	0.2	948	0.3
Hindi	95	—	866	2.2	56	0.5	50	0.4	13	—	1,080	0.4
Urdu	6	—	6	—	—	—	1,162	9.3	—	—	1,174	0.4
Other	1,524	0.8	132	0.4	44	0.4	527	4.2	892	2.6	3,119	1.1
Not speaking yet	1,124	0.6	634	1.6	226	2.1	364	2.9	709	2.1	3,057	1.1
Not stated	75	—	12	—	38	0.3	—	—	49	0.1	174	0.1
Total	188,923	100	39,743	100	10,808	100	12,434	100	34,112	100	286,020	100

IV Appendices

Table 6 Religion by ward

Ward abbreviation	Ward	Religion											Not stated		Total population	
		Christian		Hindu		Sikh		Muslim		Other		No religion					
		Number	%	Number	%	Number	%	Number	%	Number	%	Number	%	Number	%	Number	%
AB	Abbey	4,403	46.1	4,204	44.0	361	3.8	174	1.8	19	0.2	399	4.2	—	—	9,560	100
AY	Aylestone	9,409	86.9	112	1.0	50	0.5	—	—	94	0.9	1,121	10.4	44	0.4	10,830	100
BL	Beaumont Leys	8,471	68.0	934	7.5	25	0.2	392	3.1	336	2.7	2,242	18.0	56	0.4	12,456	100
BE	Belgrave	5,606	44.0	5,325	41.8	585	4.6	542	4.3	62	0.5	610	4.8	6	—	12,736	100
CA	Castle	6,440	63.2	436	4.3	442	4.3	367	3.6	81	0.8	2,298	22.6	118	1.2	10,182	100
CW	Charnwood	4,746	39.2	2,765	22.8	1,837	15.2	1,706	14.1	69	0.6	990	8.2	—	—	12,113	100
CO	Coleman	6,010	71.5	710	8.4	536	6.4	56	0.7	118	1.4	934	11.1	44	0.5	8,408	100
CH	Crown Hills	3,425	34.9	3,552	36.2	1,526	15.5	878	8.9	43	0.4	367	3.7	24	0.2	9,815	100
EK	East Knighton	7,043	75.7	125	1.3	143	1.5	100	1.1	118	1.3	1,669	17.9	106	1.1	9,305	100
EV	Evington	7,734	86.7	81	0.9	125	1.4	149	1.7	181	2.0	629	7.0	25	0.3	8,924	100
EM	Eyres Monsell	8,750	84.0	—	—	25	0.2	6	0.1	137	1.3	1,470	14.1	25	0.2	10,413	100
HU	Humberstone	8,545	81.4	187	1.8	6	0.1	56	0.5	56	0.5	1,625	15.5	19	0.2	10,494	100
LA	Latimer	2,435	33.0	4,416	59.8	93	1.3	162	2.2	25	0.3	255	3.5	—	—	7,386	100
MM	Mowmacre	5,848	82.5	81	1.1	19	0.3	62	0.9	93	1.3	978	13.8	6	0.1	7,087	100
NP	New Parks	10,294	89.3	37	0.3	—	—	19	0.2	69	0.6	1,109	9.6	—	—	11,528	100
NB	North Braunstone	7,397	82.9	25	0.3	—	—	50	0.6	69	0.8	1,277	14.3	106	1.2	8,924	100
RF	Rowley Fields	7,293	81.3	492	5.5	380	4.2	50	0.6	93	1.0	648	7.2	18	0.2	8,974	100
RM	Rushey Mead	5,469	43.5	5,200	41.3	1,171	9.3	280	2.2	62	0.5	380	3.0	18	0.1	12,580	100
SF	Saffron	9,279	86.1	69	0.6	87	0.8	12	0.1	19	0.2	1,302	12.1	6	0.1	10,774	100
SA	St. Augustines	6,938	72.9	741	7.8	181	1.9	12	0.1	62	0.7	1,563	16.4	19	0.2	9,516	100
SH	Spinney Hill	2,441	23.7	2,989	29.0	579	5.6	3,706	36.0	56	0.5	486	4.7	50	0.5	10,307	100
ST	Stoneygate	4,609	54.0	1,407	16.5	847	9.9	411	4.8	137	1.6	1,090	12.8	37	0.4	8,538	100
TC	Thurncourt	9,273	84.3	62	0.6	25	0.2	187	1.7	31	0.3	1,376	12.5	44	0.4	10,998	100
WC	Westcotes	5,756	53.6	1,594	14.9	797	7.4	230	2.1	268	2.5	2,049	19.1	37	0.3	10,731	100
WP	Western Park	10,178	87.3	386	3.3	87	0.7	87	0.7	49	0.4	847	7.3	31	0.3	11,665	100
WH	West Humberstone	5,911	66.1	1,351	15.1	280	3.1	374	4.2	25	0.3	990	11.1	12	0.1	8,943	100
WK	West Knighton	8,289	85.0	305	3.1	262	2.7	37	0.4	19	0.2	785	8.1	50	0.5	9,747	100
WY	Wycliffe	5,468	50.3	1,825	16.8	249	2.3	2,217	20.4	131	1.2	965	8.9	19	0.2	10,874	100
	Total	187,460	66.1	39,411	13.9	10,718	3.8	12,322	4.3	2,522	0.9	30,454	10.7	920	0.3	283,807	100

IV Appendices

Map 1 Hindus in Leicester (1983)

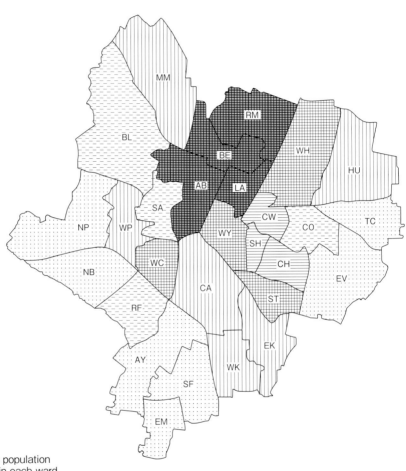

Key to % of the population
who are Hindu in each ward.

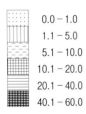

0.0 – 1.0
1.1 – 5.0
5.1 – 10.0
10.1 – 20.0
20.1 – 40.0
40.1 – 60.0

IV Appendices

[2001 Census]

Table 1 Ethnicity in the UK and Leicester

Ethnic group	UK		Leicester	
	Population	%	Population	%
White	54,153,898	92.1	178,739	63.9
British	50,366,497	85.67	169,456	60.54
Irish	691,232	1.2	3,602	1.29
Other White	3,069,169	5.27	5,681	2.03
Mixed	677,117	1.2	6,506	2.3
White & Black Caribbean	———	—	2,841	1.01
White & Black African	———	—	539	0.19
White & Asian	———	—	1,908	0.68
Other Mixed	———	—	1,218	0.44
Asian or Asian British	2,311,423	4.0	83,751	29.9
Indian	1,053,411	1.8	72,033	25.73
Pakistani	747,285	1.3	4,276	1.53
Bangladeshi	283,063	0.5	1,926	0.69
Other Asian	247,664	0.4	5,516	1.97
Black or Black British	1,148,738	2.0	8,595	3.1
Caribbean	565,876	1.0	4,610	1.65
African	485,277	0.8	3,432	1.23
Other Black	97,585	0.2	553	0.2
Chinese	247,403	0.4	1,426	0.51
Other Ethnic Group	230,615	0.4	904	0.32
Total	58,789,194	100	279,921	100

Table 2 Religion in the UK and Leicester

Religion	UK		Leicester	
	Population	%	Population	%
Christian	42,079,000	71.6	125,187	44.7
Buddhist	152,000	0.3	638	0.2
Hindu	559,000	1.0	41,248	14.7
Jewish	267,000	0.5	417	0.2
Muslim	1,591,000	2.7	30,885	11.0
Sikh	366,000	0.6	11,796	4.2
Other religion	179,000	0.3	1,179	0.4
No religion	9,104,000	15.5	48,798	17.4
Religion not stated	4,289,000	7.3	19,782	7.0
Total	58,789,000	100	279,921	100

Ⅳ Appendices

Map 1 Hindu population in the towns in the UK (Over 5,000 Hindus)

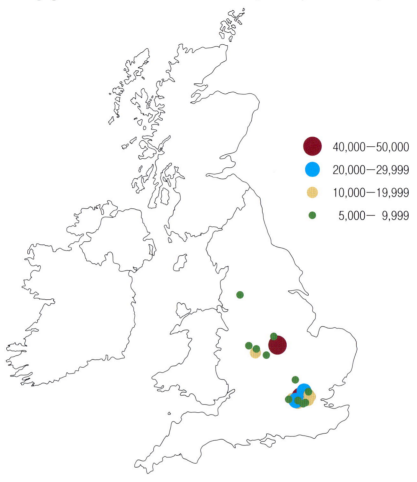

Local authority	Population	%	Local authority	Population	%
Brent	45,228	17.2	Wolverhampton	9,198	3.9
Leicester	41,248	14.7	Enfield	9,176	3.4
Harrow	40,548	19.6	Merton	8,736	4.6
Ealing	23,384	7.8	Coventry	7,757	2.6
Barnet	21,011	6.7	Charnwood	6,105	4.0
Birmingham	19,358	2.0	Wandsworth	5,929	2.3
Redbridge	18,661	7.8	Sandwell	5,577	2.0
Newham	16,901	6.9	Kingston upon Thames	5,343	3.6
Croydon	16,781	5.1	Slough	5,340	4.5
Hounslow	16,064	7.6	Bolton	5,232	2.0
Hillingdon	11,197	4.6	Luton	5,025	2.7

IV Appendices

Table 3 Religion in Leicester

Ward abbreviation	Ward	Christian		Hindu		Muslim		Sikh		Buddist		Jewish		Other religions	
		Number	%	Number	%	Number	%	Number	%	Number	%	Number	%	Number	%
AB	Abbey	7,184	56.51	1,172	9.22	275	2.16	337	2.65	27	0.21	6	0.05	52	0.41
AY	Aylestone	7,051	65.28	220	2.04	137	1.27	65	0.60	21	0.19	5	0.05	27	0.25
BL	Beaumont Leys	7,530	54.42	1,067	7.71	557	4.03	193	1.39	49	0.35	8	0.06	44	0.32
BE	Belgrave	2,005	19.47	5,346	51.92	1,004	9.75	562	5.46	12	0.12	6	0.06	80	0.78
BP/RF	Braunstone Park & Rowley Fields	8,916	53.67	721	4.34	306	1.84	578	3.48	21	0.13	8	0.05	66	0.40
CA	Castle	6,394	47.49	594	4.41	931	6.91	343	2.55	148	1.10	65	0.48	88	0.65
CW	Charnwood	4,142	38.84	1,296	11.90	2,288	21.46	400	3.75	17	0.16	6	0.06	48	0.45
CO	Coleman	3,669	30.32	2,577	21.30	2,890	23.88	1,082	8.94	14	0.12	3	0.02	20	0.17
EV	Evington	4,918	50.25	1,632	16.67	874	8.93	941	9.61	8	0.08	13	0.13	35	0.36
EM	Eyres Monsell	7,079	63.05	92	82.00	113	1.01	35	0.31	11	0.10	0	0.00	22	0.20
FO	Fosse	6,234	58.07	635	5.92	269	2.51	195	1.82	16	0.15	9	0.08	35	0.33
FR	Freemen	5,597	56.07	190	1.90	190	1.90	123	1.23	41	0.41	14	0.14	45	0.45
HU/HA	Humberstone & Hamilton	6,768	56.91	1,604	13.49	353	2.97	434	3.65	6	0.05	6	0.05	41	0.34
KN	Knighton	9,087	55.87	1,247	7.67	628	3.86	1,103	6.78	59	0.36	161	0.99	76	0.47
LA	Latimer	1,527	13.18	7,642	65.98	839	7.24	432	3.73	15	0.13	4	0.03	49	0.42
NP	New Parks	9,922	61.93	430	2.68	105	0.66	86	0.54	17	0.11	7	0.04	45	0.28
RM	Rushey Mead	4,564	30.16	6,203	40.99	838	5.54	1,501	9.92	7	0.05	4	0.03	112	0.74
SH	Spinney Hills	3,083	14.51	3,127	14.72	11,886	55.94	885	4.16	29	0.14	16	0.08	58	0.27
ST	Stonegate	3,869	22.67	3,237	18.97	5,379	31.52	1,598	9.36	48	0.28	41	0.24	96	0.56
TC	Thurncourt	6,304	63.45	673	6.77	325	3.27	266	2.68	12	0.12	11	0.11	30	0.30
WC	Westcotes	3,689	42.63	733	8.47	493	5.70	337	3.89	38	0.44	12	0.14	71	0.82
WP	Western Park	5,655	57.17	837	8.46	205	2.07	300	3.03	22	0.22	12	0.12	39	0.39
	City of Leicester (Total)	125,187	44.7	41,248	14.7	30,885	11.0	11,796	4.2	638	0.2	417	0.2	1,179	0.4

IV Appendices

Map 2 Hindus in Leicester

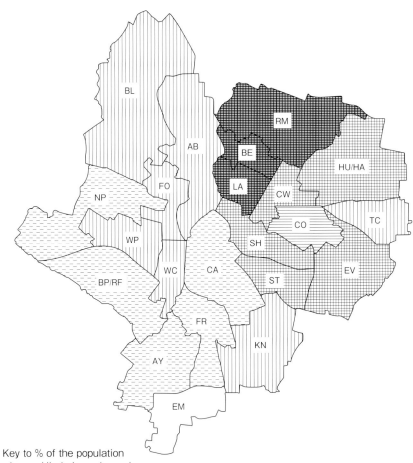

Key to % of the population who are Hindu in each ward.

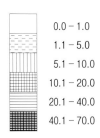

0.0 – 1.0
1.1 – 5.0
5.1 – 10.0
10.1 – 20.0
20.1 – 40.0
40.1 – 70.0

IV Appendices

[2011 Census]

Table 1 Ethnicity in Leicester and 'England and Wales'

Ethnic group	Leicester		England and Wales
	Population	%	%
White: UK	148,629	45.1	80.5
Irish	2,524	0.8	0.9
Other White	15,066	4.6	4.4
Gypsy or Irish Traveller	417	0.1	0.1
Mixed: White and Black Caribbean	4,691	1.4	0.8
White and Black African	1,161	0.4	0.3
White and Asian	3,388	1.0	0.6
Other Mixed	2,340	0.7	0.5
Asian or Asian British: Indian	93,335	28.3	2.5
Pakistani	8,067	2.4	2.0
Bangladeshi	3,642	1.1	0.8
Other Asian	13,181	4.0	1.5
Black or Black British: Caribbean	4,790	1.5	1.1
African	12,480	3.8	1.8
Other Black	3,315	1.0	0.5
Chinese	4,245	1.3	0.7
Other Ethnic Groups: Arab	3,311	1.0	0.4
Any other ethnic group	5,257	1.6	0.6

Table 2 Religion in Leicester and England

Religion	Leicester		England
	Population	%	%
Christian	106,872	32.4	59.4
Buddhist	1,224	0.4	0.5
Hindu	50,087	15.2	1.5
Jewish	295	0.1	0.5
Muslim	61,440	18.6	5.0
Sikh	14,457	4.4	0.8
Other religions	1,839	0.6	0.4
No religion	75,280	22.8	24.7
Religion not stated	18,345	5.6	7.2

IV   Appendices

Appendix 11: Maps of the Gujarat state of India, Germany and Leicester in the UK

1   Gujarat state of India

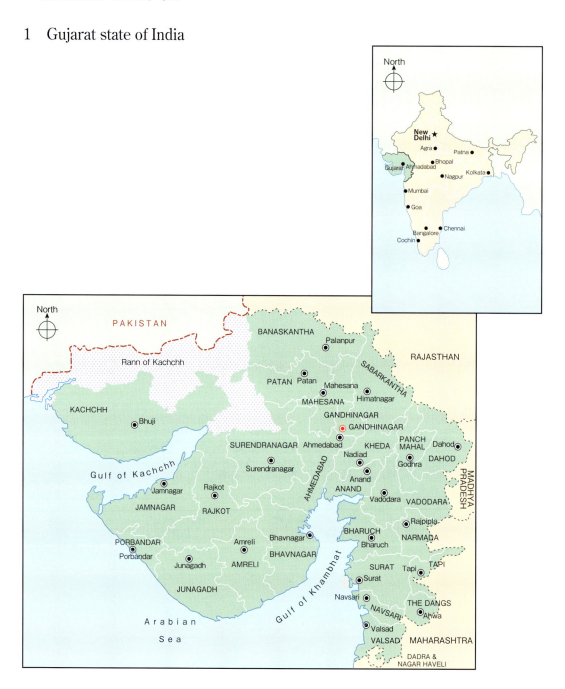

IV Appendices

2 Germany

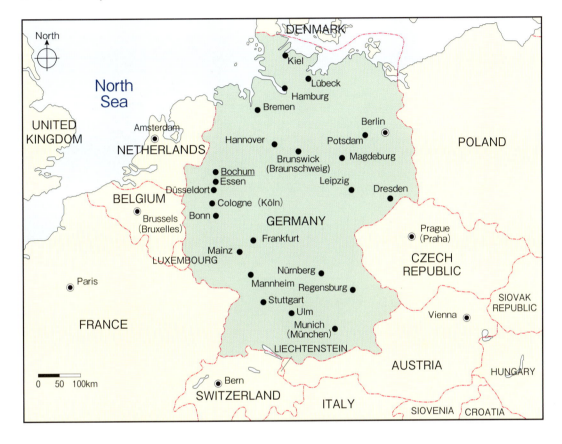

IV Appendices

3 Leicester

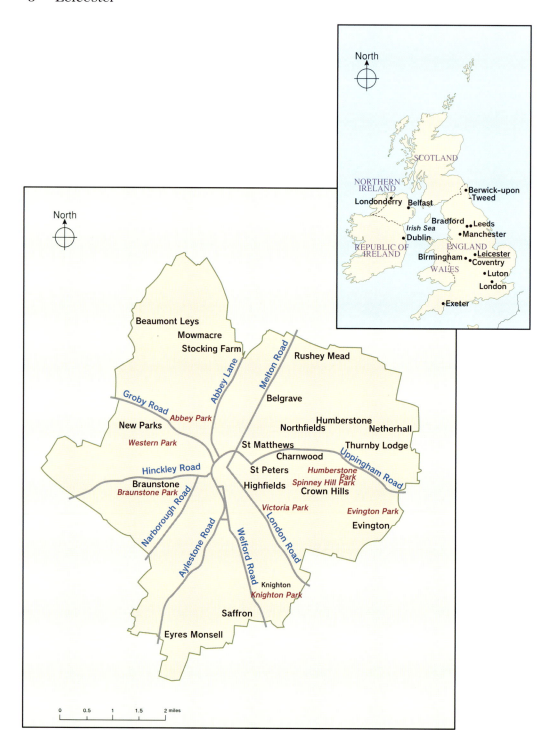

Appendix 12: Select bibliography and websites

Hinduism and Indian laws

- Burnett, David, G., *The Spirit of Hinduism: A Christian Perspective on Hindu Life & Thought*, 2nd ed., Oxford: Monarch Books, 2006.
- Clothey, Fred W., *Religion in India: A Historical Introduction*, London & New York: Routledge, 2006.
- Hopkins, T. J., *The Hindu Religious Tradition*, Encino: Dickenson Publishing Company, 1971.
- Johnson, W. J., *Oxford Dictionary of Hinduism*, Oxford: Oxford University Press, 2009.
- Kanitkar, V. P. Hermant & Cole, Owen, *Hinduism: An Introduction*, 3rd ed., London: Teach Yourself, 2010.
- Klostermaier, Klaus K., *A Short History of Hinduism*, Oxford: Oneworld, 2000.
- Lal, Brij V. (ed.), *The Encycropedia of the Indian Diaspora*, Honolulu: University of Hawaii Press, 2006.
- Menski, Werner, 'Einwanderer in Großbritannien'. In: *anglistik und englischunterricht* 10, 1980, 125-138.
- Menski, Werner, 'From alu ke paraunthe to Jain law'. In Bhattacharya, N. N. (ed.): *Jainism and Prakrit in Ancient and Medieval India. Essays for Prof. Jagdish Chandra Jain*. New Delhi: Manohar, 1993, 23-30.
- Menski, Werner, *Modern Indian Family Law*, Richmond: Curzon Press, 2000.
- Menski, Werner, *Hindu Law: Beyond Tradition and Modernity*, New Delhi: Oxford University Press, 2003.
- Rodrigues, Hilary P., *Introducing Hinduism*, London & New York, Routledge, 2006.
- Sen, K. M., *Hinduism*, Harmondsworth: Penguin Books, 1961.
- Seshagiri, Rao, K. L. (chief ed.), *Encycopedia of Hinduism*, 11 vols., Mandala Pub., 2013.
- Stutley, M., *Hinduism: the Eternal Law*, Wellingborough: Aquarian Press, 1985.
- Williams, Raymond Bradley (ed.), *A Sacred Thread: Modern Transmission of Hindu Traditions in India and Abroad*, New York: Columbia University Press, 1996.
- Zaehner, R. C., *Hinduism*, London: Oxford University Press, 1962.
- Zavos, John, Kanungo, Pralay, Reddy, Deepa S., Warrier, Maya & Williams, Raymond Brady (eds), *Public Hinduisms*, London: SAGE, 2012.

South Asian Dance

- Coomaraswamy, Ananda, *The Mirror of Gesture*. New Delhi: Munshiram Manoharlal. (An English translation of the ancient text Abhinayadarpanam), 1977.
- David, Ann R., *Performing Faith: Dance, Identity and Religion in Hindu Communities in Leicester and London*. Leicester: De Montfort University. (Unpublished PhD thesis), 2005.
- David, Ann R., 'Beyond the Silver Screen: Bollywood and Filmi Dance in the UK', *South Asia Research*, 27(1), 2007, 5-24.

IV Appendices

- Grau, Andrée, 'Political Activism and South Asian Dance: The case of Mallika Sarabhai', *South Asia Research*, 27(1), 2007, 43-55.
- Hyde, Colin, Vadnerkar, Smita & Cutting, Angela (ed.), *Parampara – Continuing the Tradition: Thirty Years of Indian Dance and Music in Leicester*, Leicester: Leicester City Council, 1996.
- Brown, Cynthia & Menski, Werner, *Karman: History of South Asian Dance in Leicester and Leicestershire*, 2012, Leicester: Centre for Indian Classical Dance (CICD).
- Khan, Naseem, *The Arts Britain Ignores: The Arts of Ethnic Minorities in Britain*. London: Community Relations Commission, 1976.
- Prickett, Stacey, '*Guru* or Teacher? *Shishya* or Student? Pedagogic Shifts in South Asian Dance Training in Indian and Britain', *South Asia Research*, 27(1), 2007, 25-41.
- *Sinjini* (Educational DVD), Leicester: CICD, 2007.

South Asians in the UK, mainly Hindus

- Ali, N., Kalra, V. S. & Sayyid, S. (eds), *A Postcolonial People: South Asians in Britain*, London: Hurst & Company, 2006.
- Badham, Paul (ed.), *Religion, State, and Society in Modern Britain*, Lampeter: Edwin Mallen Press, 1989.
- Ballard, R. (ed.), *Desh Pardesh: The South Asian Presence in Britain*, London: Hurst & Company, 1994 (2006).
- Baumann, Gerd, *Contesting Culture: Discourses of Identity in Multi-Ethnic London*, Cambridge: Cambridge University Press, 1996.
- Bowen, D. (ed.), *Hinduism in England*, Bradford: Bradford College, 1981.
- Brown, Callum G., *Religion and Society in Twentieth-Century Britain*, London: MacHarlow: Pearson Longman, 2006.
- Brown, Judith B. & Foot, Rosemary (eds), *Migration: The Asian Experience*, Basingstoke: Macmillan, 1994.
- Burghart R. (ed.), *Hinduism in Great Britain: The Perpetuation of Religion in an Alien Cultural Milieu*, London: Tavistock, 1987.
- Coward, Harold, Hinnells, John R. & Williams, Raymond Brady (eds), *The South Asian Religious Diaspora in Britain, Canada, and the United States*, New York: State University of New York Press, 2000.
- Desai, R., *Indian Immigrants in Britain*, London: Oxford University Press, 1963.
- Firth, S., *Death, Dying and Bereavement in a British Hindu Community*, Kampen: Kok Pharos, 1997.
- Harrison, S. W., *Hinduism in Preston*, Preston: S. Harrison, 1978.
- Heath, Deana & Mathur, Chandana (eds), *Communalism and Globalization in South Asia and its Diaspora*, London: Routledge, 2011.
- Jackson, Robert & Nesbitt, Eleanor, *Hindu Children in Britain*, Stoke-on-Trent: Trentham Books, 1993.
- Kanitkar, H. & Jackson, R, *Hindus in Britain*, London: University of London (SOAS), 1982.

- Knott, Kim, *Hinduism in Leeds: A Study of Religious Practices in the Indian Hindu Community and in Hindu-Related Groups*, Leeds: Community Religious Project at the University of Leeds, 1986.
- Lahiri, Shompa, *Indians in Britain: Anglo-Indian Encounters, Race and Identity 1880-1930*, London: Frank Cass, 2000.
- Menski, Martin, *Reconceptualising the Geography of the Asian Niche Market: A Critical Analysis of the Viability of Asian Retail Businesses in the UK*. London: SOAS (unpublished Geography ISP Dissertation), 2001.
- Morgan, Peggy & Lawton, Clive A., *Ethical Issues in Six Religious Traditions*, Edinburgh: Edinburgh University Press, 2007.
- Nasta, Susheila (ed.), *India in Britain: South Asian Networks and Connections, 1858-1950*, Basingstoke: Palgrave Macmillan, 2013.
- Nesbitt, Eleanor, *My Dad's Hindu, My Mum's Side Are Sikhs: Issues in Religious Identity*, Charlbury: National Foundation for Arts Education, 1991.
- Nesbitt, Eleanor, *Interfaith Pilgrims: Living Truths and Truthful Living*, London: Quaker Books, 2003.
- Nesbitt, Eleanor, *Intercultural Education: Ethnographic and Religious Approaches*, Brighton: Sussex Academic Press, 2004.
- Pocock, D. F., 'Preservation of the Religious Life: Hindu Immigrants in England', *Contributions to Indian Sociology* (New Series), vol. 10, no. 2, 1976, 341-365.
- Ranasinha, Ruvani (ed.), *South Asians and Shaping of Britain, 1870-1950: A Sourcebook*, Manchester: Manchester University Press, 2012.
- Shukla, Sandhya, *India Abroad: Diasporic Cultures of Postwar America and England*, Princeton: Princeton University Press, 2003.
- Tambs-Lyche, H., 'A Comparison of Gujarati Communities in London and the Midlands', *New Community*, vol. 4, no. 3, 1975, 349-355.
- Thomas, Terence (ed.), *The British: Their Religious Beliefs and Practices 1800-1986*, London & New York: Routledge, 1988.
- Thomas, Terence, 'Fragmented University: Islam and Muslims', in Parsons, Gerald (ed.), *The Growth of Religious Diversity: Britain from 1945*, vol. 1, London: Routledge, 1993.
- Vertovec, Steven, *The Hindu Diaspora: Comparative Patterns*, London & New York: Routledge, 2000.
- Visram, Rozina, *Asians in Britain: 400 Years of History*, London: Pluto Press, 2002.
- Visram, Rozina, *The History of the Asian Community in Britain*, London: Wayland Publisher, 1995.
- Wainwright, A. Martin, *'The Better Class' of Indians: Social Ran, Imperial Identity, and South Asians in Britain 1858-1914*, Manchester: Manchester University Press, 2008.
- Weller, Paul (ed.), *Religions in the UK: Directory 2001-03*, Derby: the Multi-Faith Centre at the University of Derby, 2001.
- Woodhead, Linda & Catto, Rebecca, *Religion and Change in Modern Britain*, London: Routledge, 2012.

IV Appendices

History of Leicester, including Hindus

[Books and articles]
- Bonney, Richard, *Understanding and Celebrating Religious Diversity: The Growth of Diversity in Leicester's Places of Religious Worship since 1970*, Leicester: University of Leicester, 2003.
- Brown, Cynthia, *Leicester Voices*, Stroud: Tempus, 2002.
- Burrell, Kathy, *Moving Lives: Narratives of Nation and Migration among Europeans in Post-War Britain*, Aldershot: Ashgate, 2006.
- Chessum, Lorna, *From Immigrants to Ethnic Minority: Making Black Community in Britain*, Aldershot: Ashgate, 2000.
- Daahir, Jawaahir, et. al., *Somalia to Europe: Stories of Somali Diaspora*, Leicester: Leicester Quaker Press, 2011.
- Davis, Vernon, *Leicester Celebrates: Festivals in Leicester Past & Present*, Leicester: Leicester City Council Living History Unit, 1996.
- England, Steve, *Magnificent Mercury: History of a Regional Newspaper: The First 125 Years of the Leicester Mercury*, Leicester: Kairos Press, 1999.
- Haq, Tim & Law, Bill (eds), *Belgrave Memories: 1945 to 2005*, East Midlands Economic Network, 2007.
- Herbert, Joanna, *Negotiating Boundaries in the City: Migration, Ethnicity, and Gender in Britain*, Aldershot: Ashgate, 2008.
- Jewson, Nick (ed.), *Migration Processes and Ethnic Divisions*, Leicester: Centre for Urban History/Ethnicity Research Centre, University of Leicester, 1995.
- Jordan, Christine, *The Illustrated History of Leicester's Suburbs*, Derby: Breedon Books Publishing, 2003.
- Kuepper, W. G., Lackey, G. L. & Swinerton, E. N., *Ugandan Asians in Great Britain: Forced Migration and Social Absorption*, London: Croom Helm, 1975.
- Lalani, Z. (compiled), *Ugandan Asian Expulsion: 90 Days and Beyond Through the Eyes of the International Press*, Tampa, FL: Expulsion Publications, 1997.
- Leicestershire Multicultural Archive Project, *Highfields Remembered: Memories of How a Community Developed from the First World War to Present Day*, Leicester: Leicestershire County Council, De Montfort University, 1996.
- Little, Gwyneth (ed.), *Meeting Hindus*, Leicester: Christians Aware, 2001.
- Marett, Valerie, *Immigrants Settling in the City*, Leicester: Leicester University Press, 1989.
- Marett, Valerie, 'Resettlement of Ugandan Asians in Leicester', *Journal of Refugee Studies*, vol. 6, no. 3, 1993, 248-259.
- Martin, John & Singh, Gurharpal, *Asian Leicester*, Stroud: Sutton Publishing, 2002.
- Menski, Werner, *Verteilungs-und Funktionsmerkmale des asiatischen Einzelhandels in englischen Industriestädten, dargestellt am Beispiel von Leicester*. (Distributional and functional patterns of Asian retail trade in English industrial cities, illustrated through the example of Leicester). Kiel: University of Kiel. (Unpublished MA thesis), 1977.
- Nicholson, Julia, *Traditional Indian Arts of Gujarat*, Leicester: Leicestershire

Museums Publication, 1988.
- Rooney, Yvonne & O'Connor, Henrietta, *The Spatial Distribution of Ethnic Minority Communities in Leicester, 1971, 1981 & 1991: Maps and Tables*, Leicester: Centre for Urban History/Ethnicity Research Centre, University of Leicester, 1995.
- Sato Kiyotaka (ed.), *Life Story of Mr Jaffer Kapasi, OBE: Muslim Businessman in Leicester, and the Ugandan Expulsion in 1972*, Tokyo: Research Centre for the History of Religious and Cultural Diversity (Meiji University), 2012.
- Sato Kiyotaka (ed.), *The Life Story of Mr Andrejs Ozolins, a Latvian, and His Wife Mrs Dulcie Ozolins*, Tokyo: Research Centre for the History of Religious and Cultural Diversity (Meiji University), 2014.
- Sato Kiyotaka (ed.), *The Life Story of Mr Ramanbhai Barber, MBE, DL: The President of the Shree Sanatan Mandir in Leicester*, Tokyo: Research Centre for the History of Religious and Cultural Diversity (Meiji University), 2015.
- Seliga, Joseph, 'A Neighbourhood Transformed: the Effect of Indian Migration on the Belgrave Area of Leicester, 1965-1995', *The Local Historian*, vol. 28, no. 4, 1998, 225-41.
- Singh, Gurharpal, 'A City of Surprises: Urban Multiculturalism and the "Leicester Model"', in Ali, N. Kalra, V. S. & Sayyid, S. (eds), *A Postcolonial People: South Asians in Britain*, London: Hurst & Company, 2006, 291-304.
- Smith, Michael, *The Story of Belgrave: the Life and Death of a Leicestershire Village*, Birstall: Birstall Local History Society, 2013.
- Vershinina, N., Barrett, R. & Meyer, M., *Polish Immigrants in Leicester: Forms of Underpinning Entrepreneurial Activity*, Leicester: De Montfort University, 2009.
- Walker, Penny (ed.), *We are South Highfields: Life in Our Area, Past & Present*, London: Near Neighbours, 2012.
- Wheatley, Ken, *More Memories of Leicester*, Elland (West Yorkshire): True North Books, 2000.

[Pamphlets, newspaper and others]
- *Survey of Leicester, 1983: Initial Report of Survey*, Leicester: Leicester City Council and Leicestershire County Council, 1984.
- *Survey of Leicester, 1983: Ward Tables*, Leicester: Leicester City Council and Leicestershire County Council, 1988.
- *Embracing the Present Planning the Future: Social Action by the Faith Communities of Leicester*, Leicester: Leicester Faiths Regeneration Project sponsored by Diocese of Leicester, 2004.
- *20th Anniversary Brochure for Leicester Council of Faiths*, Leicester: Leicester Council of Faiths, 2006.
- *The Diversity of Leicester: A Demographic Profile*, Leicester: Leicester City Council, 2008.
- *Leicester Migration Stories: Making Histories*, London: Runnymede, 2012.
- *Somalis in Leicester*, New York: Open Society Foundations, 2014.
- *Leicester Mercury*, 1981-2012.

IV Appendices

Websites

- Belgrave Neighbourhood Centre
  (http://www.leicester.gov.uk/your-community/community-support...)
- Diwali
  (http://www.visitleicester.info/things-to-see-and-do/festivals-celebrations/diwali/)
- Gujarat Hindu Association
  (http://www.ghauk.com/)
- Highfields area
  (http://www.storyofleicester.info/mystory/highfields/)
- From Kampala to Leicester
  (http://www.storyofleicester.info/exploreleicester/exhibitionarchive/kampala...)
- From Kampala to Leicester permanent exhibition at Newark Houses Museum
  (https://macearchive.wordpress.com/2014/02/11/from-kampala-to-leicester...)
- The Leicester Council of Faiths
  (http://www.lcof.org.uk/)

Appendix 13: Message from Mrs. Nilima Devi MBE

This particular project would never have seen the light of day without the tenacity and dedication of Professor Sato. Therefore I wish to thank him, first of all, for taking the initiative to produce this study, and for his thoughtfulness in bringing together so many different strands of what Asian dance development in Leicester and beyond has been concerned about. During the past few years, Professor Sato has come to Leicester numerous times to conduct further research and interviews, with me and many other people, to check details and discuss arrangements. The focus on my life story in relation to dance development should not and cannot distract from the fact that this has been a journey involving numerous people and institutions in several countries, reflecting the global interconnectedness of our lives today. The continued strength of Asian dance in Leicester, other parts of the UK and elsewhere is in no small measure due to such multi-level and multi-agency support, especially earlier developments in private-public partnerships, which are now part of the rich local history that Professor Sato has done so well to bring to light. An individual, however determined, engaged and visionary, cannot create what is documented in this study entirely by personal engagement and dedication. It is a joint effort, and many people in Leicester and beyond have reason to thank Professor Sato for his academic leadership in this regard.

When Cynthia Brown first suggested to Professor Sato that it might be useful to produce a study on my life story as an Indian dancer in Leicester, we were engaged in preparing *Karman*, a wider history of South Asian Dance in Leicester and Leicestershire, which was published in 2012 as part of the celebrations of 30 years of CICD, the Centre for Indian Classical Dance in Leicester, which I had founded in 1981. Since that time, our family had long-standing connections to many Japanese academics through my husband's work as a specialist in comparative law. As a family, too, we had all become interested in Japan and had seen for ourselves how intercultural communication worked in other parts of the world, including Japan. Our younger son has actually lived and worked in Japan for many years. In the present study, Professor Sato also documents that some dancers from Japan came to Leicester more than ten years ago, and I am hopeful that future connections of this kind will also be possible.

I arrived in Leicester in 1980 with a young family, after a short stay in Germany. Having left India, my country of birth, and driven by a vision to remain engaged in work on and with Kathak, the beautiful North Indian style of classical dance, I found that in Leicester at that time, there was hardly any dance teaching going on, but huge scope for development. One of our earliest students from that time, Gita Lakhlani, also comments

IV Appendices

on that situation. Meanwhile, a lot has happened, and Leicester is on the global map, not only as a city with excellent rugby and football teams, but also as a place that produces global stars for the world stage of dance. I thank Professor Sato for managing so well to convey that message, which is as much a comment on my own efforts as a reflection of the unique multicultural environment that the increasingly superdiverse city of Leicester has developed and maintained over many decades.

This study also involves my family, and my husband and our two sons have been especially supportive of this study and have accompanied my life's work in relation to dance in various ways. Without their engagement, encouragement and critiques many things would not be what they are now. Together, we have also sought to raise awareness of the multiple aspects of South Asian cultures and their global relevance. In a more practical sense, we have also aimed to create opportunities for many young people to grow into professionals in their own right and to develop as individuals and members of our community that make their own contributions to the wider public good. These kinds of efforts were acknowledged when, in 2010, Jaguar Land Rover, in association with The Birmingham Post, facilitated 23 people as Cultural Champions for Arts and Business in the Midlands, honouring individual outstanding contribution to the arts. Together with several other people from Leicester, including Peter Baker, who had earlier been leading Leicester's Knighton Fields Dance and Drama Centre, I had been nominated. This was a splendid occasion marking CICD's contributions over many years to dance and business development in Leicester. Following our 30 year celebrations in 2011 and 2012, I was then awarded an MBE for my services to dance in the Queen's New Year's Honours List of 2013. I am of course very happy and proud about that, and was also honoured to receive a Lifetime Achievement Award from the Leicester Asian Business Association (LABA) in summer 2014. All this shows that individual engagement counts and is valued, and I hope that my life story as presented here by Professor Sato will inspire others to become involved in work that they believe to be useful and conducive to making this world a better place.

Nilima Devi MBE
Leicester
30 March 2016